PowerShell

© Copyright 2018 by ___Zach Webber_ - All rights reserved.

The following book is reproduced below with the goal of providing information that is as accurate and reliable as possible. Regardless, purchasing this book can be seen as consent to the fact that both the publisher and the author of this book are in no way experts on the topics discussed within and that any recommendations or suggestions that are made herein are for entertainment purposes only. Professionals should be consulted as needed prior to undertaking any of the action endorsed herein.

This declaration is deemed fair and valid by both the American Bar Association and the Committee of Publishers Association and is legally binding throughout the United States.

Furthermore, the transmission, duplication or reproduction of any of the following work including specific information will be considered an illegal act irrespective of whether it is done electronically or in print. This extends to creating a secondary or tertiary copy of the work or a recorded copy and is only allowed with an express written consent from the Publisher. All additional rights reserved.

The information in the following pages is broadly considered to be a truthful and accurate account of facts and as such any inattention, use or misuse of the information in question by the reader will render any resulting actions solely under their purview. There are no scenarios in which the publisher or the original author of this work can be, in any fashion, deemed liable for any hardship or damages that may befall them after undertaking information described herein.

Additionally, the information in the following pages is intended only for informational purposes and should thus be thought of as universal. As befitting its nature, it is presented without assurance regarding its prolonged validity or interim quality. Trademarks are mentioned without written consent and can in no way be considered an endorsement from the trademark holder.

TABLE OF CONTENTS

POWERSHELL

The Ultimate Beginner's Guide to Learn and Understand PowerShell Programming Effectively

Introduction 3

Chapter 1: What Is the PowerShell Language? 4
    What is PowerShell? 4
    What are the things that can I do with PowerShell? 5
    The benefits of working with PowerShell 7

Chapter 2: How to Create Your Own Commands in PowerShell 9
    How does the help command work? 10
    Concepts help 11
    Aliases 12

Chapter 3: Outputs and Pipelines in PowerShell 15
    How to work with pipelines 15
    How to work with format output 18
    How to control the output 19
    How to set the output 21

Chapter 4: The Operations and Wildcards 23
    Operators that work for comparison 23
    What are the wildcards? 25
    How to work with logical operators 27
    Arithmetic operators 29

Chapter 5: Working with Strings and Quotes in PowerShell 31
    String values 31
    How to add in special characters 33
    System_String object members 35

Chapter 6: The Drives and Providers 38

    The PowerShell Providers 38

    What are the built-in drives? 40

    How to create your own drive 41

Conclusion 43

POWERSHELL

The Utmost Intermediate Course Guide in Fundamentals and Concept of PowerShell Programming

Introduction to PowerShell 47

Chapter 1: A Brief History of Scripting 49

Chapter 2: Executing Commands 53

Chapter 3: Provider Essentials 58

Chapter 4: Custom & External Commands 60

Chapter 5: Snap-Ins, Modules and adding new tools to PowerShell 65

Chapter 6: Fully Automatic: Using the Pipeline to connect commands and create powerful tools 70

Chapter 7: Objects, Properties, Tables, Methods and Formatting Data 76

Chapter 8: Practical Applications: Multitasking and Remote Functions 86

Conclusion 93

POWERSHELL

21 Sample Codes and Advanced Crash Course Guide in Powershell Programming

Introduction 97

Chapter 1: PowerShell Commands 98

Chapter 2: Filtering and Formatting Code 105

Chapter 3: Parameter authentication 107

    authenticatelength() 108

    authenticatescript() 108

    authenticatecount() 109

    authenticaterange() 110

    authenticateset() 110

    authenticatenotvoidorclear() 111

Chapter 4: Supporting Whatif and Affirm 113

Chapter 5: Try/Catch in Powershell 119

    Try 119

    Catch 120

    Finally 121

Chapter 6: Pipeline Input for Powershell 123

Chapter 7: Using Pester with Powershell 126

    So, what is pester? 126

    Types of trialing 127

    When you should trial 128

    Running trials 129

    The First Trial 130

    The failure 132

    Allowing more than you should 133

    Pester context 133

Chapter 8: Advanced Pester trialing 137
    Let's play pretend 137
    Integration trial with $trialdrive 139
    Acceptance trials 142

Chapter 9: Abstract Code – Tree 144

Chapter 10: JSON and Powershell 148

Chapter 11: Automating a SQL Server 151

Conclusion 156

PowerShell

The Ultimate Beginner's Guide to Learn and Understand PowerShell Programming Effectively

Introduction

The following chapters will discuss everything that you need to know to get started with the PowerShell program. This is a powerful coding language that comes from Microsoft, so you know that it will work out well for you and will help you to get the total control over your computer that you are looking for. This guidebook will provide you with all the information that you need to get started with PowerShell.

There are a lot of things that you will be able to do with PowerShell, and if you like working with Windows programs, you will find that there is nothing better to work with than PowerShell. This guidebook will talk about some of the different things that you can do with PowerShell such as working with the commands, working with pipelines, and even how to work with directories. When you are done with this guidebook, you will be able to write some of your own codes in PowerShell and be able to get your computer to behave the way that you would like.

When you are ready to take control of your computer and see some great results with coding, make sure to check out this guidebook to see some good results.

There are plenty of books on this subject on the market, so thanks again for choosing this one! Every effort was made to ensure it is full of as much useful information as possible, please enjoy!

Chapter 1

What Is the PowerShell Language?

The world of coding can be an exciting place. There are a lot of languages that you can learn about and use. While people who have never worked with coding in the past may think that programming is confusing, learning a new coding language is similar to learning a new language like Greek or German. You will start out this process by learning some of the basic words that will get the language to go and how to form sentences (which will be known as 'commands' in this language) to get them to work well. This does take some time to learn, and some are easier to work with than others, but with some practice, coding can be so easy for you to work with.

For this guidebook, we will spend our time looking at the PowerShell language for Microsoft. This is basically the new 'Command Line Interface' that you can use on the Windows system. If you are familiar with how the Windows system works and you like using this, then PowerShell is a great coding language to work with. It relies on the simple Microsoft interface that you have come to know and love and it still has all the power that you are looking for to get things done. Now, let's take a look at how to get started with PowerShell and how to make it work for your coding needs.

What is PowerShell?

The first question that you may have about PowerShell is, 'What exactly is it?' PowerShell is a shell (an interactive user interface with an operating system) that Microsoft developed to help with task automation as well as configuration management. This shell is pretty powerful, and it is based on the .NET framework. It comes with the command line shell and a scripting language so that you can employ different tools to accomplish tasks that you would like to get done. PowerShell also comes with a Windows ISE to help you to create scripts without needing to type in the commands all the time.

To keep things simple, PowerShell is basically a command line interface that works with the Windows system. There are a lot of different parts that come with the PowerShell:

- Access to the Dynamic Linked Libraries with Windows
- Access to the Windows COM
- Access to Windows Management Instrumentation
- Access to the .NET Framework API
- PowerShell Functions
- PowerShell Commands
- Existing Windows Command Line Tools

There are many features that you can use when you are working with PowerShell. This system also works with other APIs as well as other technologies that you can already find on the Windows systems. This is one of the many reasons why PowerShell has become so popular. In addition, PowerShell is already included on your Windows System. For those who are on Windows 2008 or Windows 7, you will have the v2 version, and those who have newer models will have the v3 version. If you would like to change which version of PowerShell you have, you can do this on the Microsoft website.

What are the things that can I do with PowerShell?

While it is likely that you already have PowerShell on your computer if you possess a Windows computer, you may be curious to know what are the things you can do with this coding language. PowerShell is really easy to learn, and it comes with a ton of features that work well with the Windows operating system which will definitely keep you busy.

PowerShell was originally designed to help you automate and solve many hard and tedious admin tasks that are present on your computer. For example, you can use this language to look at all of the USB devices that are installed on any of the computers that are in your network. You can also set up some tasks that take you a lot of time to complete and have them work in the background while you complete other tasks. Some people will use the PowerShell to identify and kill processes that do not respond well, or you can filter out some information about your computer on your network before you export it all to the HTML format.

That is just the beginning of what you can do when you work with PowerShell. It is also possible to simplify and automate some of the tasks that you are supposed to do as an admin. This coding language can be used to create some scripts for these tasks and then can combine together a few commands to make things easier.

Many administrators of a network will use PowerShell to help them with the 'Active Directory.' Since PowerShell can hold onto hundreds of commands and you have the access to customize them, the help that PowerShell can provide ensures that you will be able to make your network more efficient and more productive.

To keep things simple, you can use PowerShell to make running your network easier, without having to waste so much time and energy on doing these tasks. While some other programming languages promise to do this, none will be as effective as PowerShell to get the work done. Add that it works well with your Windows systems, and you have the program that you need to get things done.

The benefits of working with PowerShell

There are a lot of different options that you can work with when you are ready to start coding. You can work with Python which is considered one of the easiest coding languages. There is Java or JavaScript which work well if you want to create great websites, and so much more. So, why should you choose to go with the PowerShell program? Some of the benefits of going with PowerShell over some of the other coding languages include:

- **Easy to use and fast**

PowerShell is a fast language that is really simple to use. This makes it easy for beginners to use so they can learn how to make their coding better than ever before.

- **Works with Windows**

If you have worked with Windows in the past and are a fan of the operating system, you will find that PowerShell works well with it. This helps to give you all the security and features that you are looking for in a coding language.

- **Small codes**

Many coding languages will require you to write out a huge code to do anything. You could fill out a whole page or more to do one thing, and when you try to write out a whole code, you will have to spend a lot of time and take up a lot of space. This is not true when you are working with PowerShell. Most of the codes in this programming language only require the use of just a few words to work it out, which means you can write out a whole code with only a few lines.

- **Already downloaded on your computer**

If you use a Windows computer, you will see that PowerShell is already downloaded. But if your computer doesn't have the version that you would like to work with, you can visit the Microsoft store to get that changed. But all Windows computers now come with

PowerShell and the ISE that you need to make it work so you can get started with coding in no time.

As you can see, working with PowerShell has a lot of benefits that are great when you are trying to get started on learning how to code. You can write all the codes that you are looking for without all the hard work, and you get to rely on the great Microsoft and Windows products that you have come to know and love. So, let's get started learning how to make PowerShell work for all your coding needs.

Chapter 2

How to Create Your Own Commands in PowerShell

If you would like PowerShell to work for you, it is important that you learn how to work with the commands that come with it. These commands tell the computer how you would like it to behave. Without the proper command, the program is not going to have any idea how to perform the functions that you want it to perform. Working with commands in PowerShell is pretty simple, and you will catch on quickly.

The naming convention in PowerShell is that you have to write it in the verb-noun form. This helps to keep things consistent, and it can help you to learn it faster while opening up the possibilities of expanding this later on. The 'verb' is the action part of your command, and then the 'noun' will tell the command where the action should be performed. To get the command to run in this system, you have to bring up the command prompt, similar to what you would see with Linux or some of the other operating systems, type in the requirements using the syntax that we gave above, and then press 'enter.' If you did the process right, you should see the right outcome come up.

There are times when you may forget the command that you would like to use when you are working with PowerShell. This will happen as you are learning the system or if you want to bring out a command that you do not use all that often. The good news is that there is a simple way that you can find the command that you would like to use. The 'Get' command will be there to help you out in this situation.

By using the Get command, you are telling the system that you would like to see the full list of commands that are available for you to use. You will then see a list of all the commands that you can use in PowerShell, making it much easier to find the one that you want to use. This is a tool that you will use often, especially in the beginning, to help you to learn some new codes or to help you remember a code if you forget it. If you would like to take it a little further and figure out what all the commands can do, you just need to use the 'Get Help' command to make this happen.

How does the help command work?

When you are working with PowerShell, you will notice that you can use a sequence of help files that will guide you whenever you need them. It is easy to access these help files by using the command 'Get-Help.' Once the system reads this command, it will bring up all the commands that are available in this system as well as their descriptions, so you know how each one will work. This can be good if you really have no idea how to use the commands or which command you would need to put into your code.

Notice that when you use this command, there is a hyphen that shows up between the verb and the noun to help separate them and to let the command prompt know what you would like to do. It is important that you set up all of the commands this way so that the prompt will know what you want and will bring you the information that you are requesting.

Let's see how this will all work with some other common tasks that you would need to do as the administrator. We will have a look at some commands that would help you out with some text files. First, if you have a file on your system that you would like to read through, the command that you should use is 'Get-Content.' If this is the only file that is on your system, it will show up after you placed and entered this into the command prompt.

Now, there are times when you will have more than one single text file on your computer. If you use the command that we had before, the computer will be confused as to which file you would like to look at, and it will not know what to bring you. This has a simple fix because you just need to add a few more details to make it all work. Make sure that you know what the name of the chosen text file is and then bring up your command prompt. You would then type in the command 'Get-Help name Get-Content.' This will return the command description and the syntax information. Keep in mind that the part of the Get-Content command will also return the contents of an item or return any type of file on the system to the right place.

It is easy to go through this and change up the syntax to get it to bring up any file that you would like on your system. You can have it bring up text on whatever document you would like to read, bring up files that are on other systems, and more based on the syntax and the names that you add to the code. This allows you to have a ton of freedom when you are working with commands on PowerShell and will help you to get things done the way that you would like.

Concepts help

As you are working with PowerShell, there may be times when you would like to get an overview of the concepts that are found in this coding language. To do this, you can look through the right files to find out the information that you want. Each file will begin with 'about,' and then it will end with whatever topic you are looking for. For example, you could look at the complete list of these topics just by entering the command 'Get-Help about*.'

If you type in the code that you saw above, you will just get a complete list of all the concepts that are on the computer, but this could be a long list. And if you already know the name of the file that you would like to use, it might get tedious. To make this easier, you simply need to add in the name as the parameter value in that syntax that we discussed before, and it will show up for you. The command that you need in this situation is 'Get-Help about flow control.' The command prompt will handle the rest.

Aliases

You may also want to work with what is known as 'aliases.' You may find that some of the commands you would like to use in PowerShell are longer, and if you have to spend so much time typing them out, it can get a little bit tedious. The good news is that the PowerShell system will make it easier for you by allowing aliases to refer back to some commands that you would like to use. These aliases are just alternate names that you can give to your commands. These aliases will take up less time and space than the original command, so they are like a shortcut.

You can choose between using these commands and writing down the alias that you would like to use. If you would like to use an alias for your code, you can just type in 'Get-Alias.' This will tell the command prompt that you want to see the aliases that you would like to use and it can save you some time.

Now, for a bit of clarification, it is important to note that the current session will refer to the current connection with PowerShell. When you first open up PowerShell, a brand new session will be created. This session will remain in effect until you close and exit out of PowerShell, which will effectively end the connection as well as the session. One thing that you can do during your sessions on PowerShell is to look under Get-Alias and see what other aliases were created by users during that session as well as any aliases that are defined in the startup, user configurations, or profiles.

If you would like to view a specified command alias, you will have to identify the specific 'Get-Alias' command. For example, if you would like to view the aliases that you can use with 'Get-ChildItem,' you will need to enter the following command:

Get-Alias |

Where-Object {$_.definition

-match "Get-ChildItem"}

At this point, you probably feel confused as you look at the code because there are some commands in there that you do not understand. We will go through those a bit more throughout the guidebook, but the part that is important right now is that the outcome you get from this command is directed to the 'Where-Object' command. This allows you to filter out any results that are not matching up with what you would like. It is possible to do this with any alias or command that you want. You simply need to go through and change the name around to what you are looking for.

One thing to note here is that PowerShell will utilize three aliases when it is working with the Get-ChildItem, and these would include *ls*, *gci*, and *dir*. Each of these will provide you with the same results so you can use the one that you would like. So, the three codes that we wrote below will work the same way, so you get the choice of which one to go with:

Get-ChildItem c:/windows

dir c:/windows

ls c:/windows

gci c:/windows

If you are feeling a bit adventurous, you can create one of your own aliases inside the current session by using the command 'Set-Alias.' It is pretty easy to do. So, let's say that you want to create an alias for Get-Content and you want to name it *cnt*. All you have to do is run the command *"Set-Alias cnt Get-Content."*

As you can see from the example above, you have created a new alias, and you could use the shortcut *cnt* any time that you want to use the Get-Content command in the system. This new alias that you created will stay active until you end that session in PowerShell or when you exit out of the system. If you accidentally exit the program and you want to use that alias again when you write another code, this is easy to do.

As you can see, working with the command language in PowerShell is not meant to be difficult. Many coding languages are hard to work with, and you may spend many weeks or longer trying to learn just the basics that go with it. However, you will find that even as a beginner, working with PowerShell is easy and you can catch up with using the syntax and the commands in no time.

Chapter 3

Outputs and Pipelines in PowerShell

Now that you have a good idea of what the commands are all about and how they will run the program, it is time to move on to something else that will help your program become more effective. Since commands won't always have the power that you need to get things done, PowerShell has created what is known as a 'pipeline' to make things easier. These pipelines are useful because they will link your commands together to accomplish more complex tasks and other things inside the code compared to what the commands can do on their own. This chapter will focus on showing you how to work with pipelines inside of PowerShell so that you can add some more power to your code.

How to work with pipelines

As we have stated in this guidebook, PowerShell is a system that is based off a set of commands. These commands can be passed on to objects with one command and be moved over to the next object the same way. Each command creates an object before it sends that object down the line so that the following command can pick it up. The next command to pick it up will then utilize the object as the input so that it can create its own output before sending that part down to the next command. This is a continuous line that will keep on going until it reaches the right conclusion. This chain of command will sometimes be really long, although there are times when it can be short, and it creates a pipeline. This is shown with the help of the (|) symbol.

In your traditional command shell, the results coming from the pipeline will all be returned at the same time. This means that the final result for your pipeline will be shown in one result rather than showing you each individual step that occurs in the pipeline. But when you are using PowerShell, you will notice that things will work a bit differently. For this one, the results will be sent through the pipeline, and when just one of the commands ends up with a result, it will be accessible right away.

Let's take a look at an example of how this works. If you are using the 'Get-Service' command, you will get a whole rundown of each service that is in the framework. Once all of this is done, you can see the command will give back the display, the admin name, and the status of the system.

To make it go further, instead of just seeing the entire rundown of the service on the system, you will get a return of the list of services that you have running and working on the system. To make this happen, you have to use both the 'Where-Object' and the 'Get-Service commands.' You would be able to use the following syntax to make this pipeline happen:

Get_Service | Where_Object {$_.status-eq 'running'}

As you have noticed, the pipeline operation is in place, and it is used to show that two commands need to be connected together. The Get-Service part of the code will produce an object that contains a full list of information that is service related. When you use this symbol, the object will then send itself over to the Where-Object command as the input. The Where-Object command will filter out that information based on what you placed into the brackets. This ensures that you will only receive back the information that you need.

Now, with this process, if the system takes a look at the information that you placed inside the brackets and determines that it is true, then the object will continue on through the pipeline. But, if there is something in the information that is seen as false, this information will be filtered out so that you only end up with the information that you actually need.

With the example that we just did, we used the operator *-eq*, which means that the status property must be equal to the running string. You must remember that you can see all of the properties you can use inside the help files while the 'Status' is a part that will generate an object with the help of the 'Get-Service' command. When you have at least one object pass through the pipeline (you can actually do more), you will be able to access the properties similar to the process you did with the Where-Object command.

Now, we will take a look at what we have to do if we wanted to limit the information that we received. Sometimes, you will get a lot of information sent back to you, and this is not a good thing if you are looking for something in particular. You do not want to spend all that time reading through the information and hoping that you will find exactly what you are looking for. The good news is that you can expand the pipeline so you can put in the right information and get the right results at the end. The syntax that you can use to make this happen is this:

Get-Service |

where {$_.status -eq 'running} |

select displayname

With the example that we listed above, the object will be received first by your Select-Object command, after it was sent there by the Where-Object command. This illustration will utilize the 'where' alias that we talked about before, so you do not need to list out the Where-Object all the time. The same thing is true when we are talking about the 'select' alias as well. This helps to shorten up the code that we are looking at a little bit and makes it easier to work with.

When you are working with all three pipelines, you must remember that you need to work on the process of operating with objects. This means that all the commands that you add to the syntax will create their own object, which will be received by the next command. The final command that you wrote will have to generate the object, which will then output the results that you are looking for.

Now that we have taken a look at how all of this will work, it is time to move on to learn how you can use these objects and their properties so that you can make refinements with your illustrations in PowerShell.

How to work with format output

Before we get too far with this option, it is important to realize that PowerShell will automatically format illustrations based on the data type that you placed in the output. So, if you use the 'Get-Process PS,' you will end up with an illustration that you can use to return any data that is found on the 'PS' process. This will display the output of the command, and if you want something else to show up, you must use the pipeline, along with a few other supported output commands, to make this happen. The four main commands that you would use to make this happen are:

- **Format-Table**

This is a command to use if you would like to show off the returned data within a table. This is often the default option that is used with many commands, so it is not always necessary that you specify the output.

- **Format-List**

This is a good command to use when you would like to return the data in a list form so that you can look at it this way.

- **Format-Wide**

This is the command that you will use to get the data to return to a wide table format. This is a table that will include just one value for each individual item that is displayed.

- **Format-Custom**

When you are using this command, you will be given data that comes from a custom format, which is based on the configuration data that you saved on the computer. When you use this format, you will notice that it comes back in the file format of *.px1xml*. Any time that you would like to update it, you can use the 'Update-Format Data' command.

How to control the output

Unless you took some special steps to override this, the default output will be applied to your format before it is sent to the console window that will show your illustration. You do have the power to override this by using the four formatting options that we talked about before. In addition to those four options that we talked about, you can also control where you send the output. Some of the commands that will make this a little bit easier include the following:

- **Out-Host**

This is the default command so you don't need to make any specifications with this one. It sends the output over to the console.

- **Out-Default**

This is another one that doesn't have to be specified in the process. It sends the output to the default formatting command that is set up. It delegates this process to the Out-Host.

- **Out-File**

This is the command that directs the output to the file you chose.

- **Out-Null**

This is the command that deletes the output. When you use this command, you will see that the PowerShell console won't show any results.

- **Out-Printer**

This is the command that will direct your output to the printer that you specified.

- **Out-String**

This is the command that will convert your object into a string array.

Remember that if you are working with your output and you need some more help controlling it, or you would like to change it up a little bit to get it to do something else, it is a good idea to use the help files to get the assistance that you need.

If you are interested in using some of the commands that are listed above, you just need to add them to the end of your pipeline. Let's take a look at an example of how this works:

Get-Process PS |

Format-List |

Out-File C:\SysInfo\ps.txt

When you use this code, you will see that the output won't be displayed on the console of PowerShell. Rather, the system will save the contents to the file that you specified in the format (you can change it as you see fit). You do need to make sure that you are sending output files that make sense. Sending some text over to a .bmp file would not make that much sense, and it will just result in an error without letting you view the output when you try to open the file later on. In addition to letting you direct the output of a file, the Out-File can be useful for allowing you to replace or append content that is already with the current output. If you do not direct it to do otherwise, the PowerShell will replace the existing content because this is the default function of the program. If you would like to append to the output file, you simply need to add the '-append' switch to this command so it would look like the following:

> *Get-Process PS |*
>
> *Format-List |*
>
> *Out-File C:\SysInfo\ps.txt*
>
> *-append*

How to set the output

The next thing that we will learn is how to set your output. In addition to making some changes in the input, there will be times when you want to control how the output works as well. You can do this with the help of the Sort-Object command. This command is in charge of taking the input of the objects of your pipeline, and it will sort them out based on the criteria that you set.

While you will usually see that PowerShell will stream the results with your pipeline's help, this command, the Sort-Object command, will wait until all of the results are retrieved, and then it will sort them out. This will stop the streaming process so that the sorting can happen first. This may not seem too big of a deal when you are starting out and when you work with smaller returns, but it will really make a difference when you are working with a ton of data at once.

Even though this command may slow down your computer, it is still one that you should know how to use. For example, if you are looking at a folder and you want to get a list of all the items that are inside, you can use the Sort-Object command to make that list. A good example of doing this is the example below where we will list out all the items that are in the C:\ Windows folder:

> *dir c:\windows |*

where {$_.length -gt 500000} |

sort -property length

-descending

With the example that we did above, the command will pass the object from the *dir* alias down to your Where-Object, which will be shown with the 'where' alias. In this command, we can specify that we wanted to get results that were larger than 500,000 (this is shown in the part for *-gt*). The object is then sent along this pipeline to the 'Sort-Object command.' When it reaches this particular part, it will start to organize based on any criteria that you listed. With this one, we added in the *-descending* to tell the system how we wanted things to show up. You can choose whether you would like to have this in or not.

Now, the formula shown above is pretty simple to work with. It will provide you with all the information that you were looking for in the system while it also goes through and makes sure that it is sorted out. Of course, you can add in some other specifications if your code needs it and the PowerShell system can be used to make these changes for you.

While it may sound complicated since you're still getting started, these pipelines can really make significant changes to the code that you are working with. They will not limit you to what you can add to the system, and you can send the object through several requirements before it shows up on the screen. This is a great way to save some time, and you can use it easily in your code, even if you are just a beginner.

Chapter 4

The Operations and Wildcards

The previous chapter was all about the pipelines that come with PowerShell and how you can use them to streamline the whole process that comes with this program. These pipelines will help you to sort out information and will make it easier to change the files that you are using. You are basically using the pipelines to connect together a string of commands so that you can filter out the objects that you want and then that information will come up on the screen.

If you have ever worked with programming in the past with another language, you have noticed that they all hold onto several operations. These operations are important because they are used to create some expressions inside of the illustration that you are making. This is something that you will see inside of PowerShell, they are just a bit different than what you will find in the other programming languages.

There are quite a few operators that are available in the PowerShell system you can use, and you have already seen some of them in the codes that we have written so far in this guidebook. Let's start out this chapter with a look at some of the operators that are available on PowerShell and how you can use them in your own commands.

Operators that work for comparison

There are a number of operators that you can use inside of your code. The first type that you may be interested in are the comparison operators. These operators follow their name and are used to compare values. During the times where your comparison is placed inside of the expression, PowerShell will compare the values that are to the left and then also the ones that are to the right of the operator. There are a lot of comparison operators that can make a difference in your code, but these are the most common ones:

- **Eq**

Equal to.

- **-ne**

Not equal to.

- **-gt**

Greater than.

- **-ge**

Greater than or equal to.

- **-lt**

Less than.

- **-le**

Less than or equal to.

- **-like**

Uses wildcards to find the matching patterns.

- **-notlike**

Uses the wildcards to find the nonmatching patterns.

- **-match**

Uses regular expressions to find matching patterns.

- **-notmatch**

Uses regular expressions to find the nonmatching patterns.

- **-contains**

Determines whether the value on the left side of your operator has the same value as the one on the right.

- **-notcontains**

Determines whether the value on the left side of the operator doesn't have the same value as the one on the right.

- **-replace**

This one will replace part or all of the value that is on the left side of the operator.

You can work with these operators to help make the comparisons that are needed inside of the PowerShell system. You will need to study each one to determine which will work for your needs. If you would like to make this system return all of the files that are in a folder and that are under a certain size, for example, you will need to work with the *-lt* operator. On the other hand, if you would like to make sure the file is larger than a chosen side, you would work with the *-gt* operator. As the programmer, you will get your choice of which operator you would like to use so make sure to choose the one that works for your codes.

What are the wildcards?

Here we will take a pause and look at what is known as the wildcards inside of PowerShell. For these, let's say that you are trying to search for an item that is in one of your files, but you are not sure about the name of the file that you want to use. This means that it is time to create a new expression that can compare a few values together. What you can do with this situation is to bring out a wildcard to use as an operator or use it as the compared value. There are a few different wildcards that you can choose to use on PowerShell including:

- (*)

This will match zero or more of any character.

- (?)

This one will match any one character that you type out.

- [char-char]

This one matches a range of sequential characters.

- [char…]

This one matches any one character in a set of characters that you defined.

These wildcards look similar to the *-notlike* and the *-like* comparison operators that we talked about earlier and they can be used to help you find whatever files you can use, even if you are unsure about which file you want to use. To see the code and understand how this should work, look at the following:

et-process |

*where {$_.company -like "*google*"}*

In the above code, the asterisk is the wildcard, and it is used to match either zero or more of the characters. This will help you get some good results, even if you are not able to pick out the exact name of the file. This is true even if the folder is stored under a different variation.

PowerShell can also complete regular expressions with our code. These regular expressions are based on the classes of regular expressions that you can easily find in the Microsoft .NET framework.

How to work with logical operators

The third type of operator that you may want to use in your code is known as 'logical operators.' So far, we are looking at operators that can create a condition and will then give us an output. However, there are times when you are working with the PowerShell program, and you have to work with expressions that have at least two conditions. This can be found when you are working with multiple comparisons that will determine whether your program should take action or stay still.

Multiple comparisons may seem complicated in the beginning, but to get them done with one expression you just need to use a logical operator and then link it to a condition. The logical operators are used to help specify what logic you would like to implement on your multiple conditions evaluation. There are several logical operators that you can work with, and these include the following:

- **-and**

This is when both conditions need to be true before the expression is evaluated as true.

- **-or**

This is when one or both conditions need to be true before the expression is evaluated as true.

- **-not**

This is when the specified condition needs to be false before the expression is evaluated as true.

- **(!)**

This is when both the conditions need to be false before the expression is evaluated as true.

To get a good understanding of how these logical operators function, let's take some time to go over the following example:

> *Get-Process |*
>
> *where {($_.handles -gt 500)*
>
> *-and ($_.pm -ne 0)}*

Let's take a look at the code above. This one is working with two conditions and both are placed inside the parentheses. With your first condition, it is used to help specify how many handles need to be bigger than the *-gt*. In this option, it is 500. In the second condition, you can specify that the paged memory won't end up being 0. You can use the logical operator to combine the two conditions together.

Since the *-and* operator is helping to connect these two expressions, both of these expressions need to be true. Only if the document or the file matches up with both of the conditions will it show up on the console. If the document will only match up with one condition or the other, they will not show up on the screen. It does not matter which condition is met and which one is not. This helps keep the amount of information that you see on the screen down to a minimum. If it does not match both of the conditions that you set, then it will not show up.

Another thing to keep in mind is that you do have the option to work with the *-or* operator. The *-or* operator can be placed into the formula like you would with the other logical operators, but they will work in a slightly different way. Let's take a look at a code and how this operator will affect it:

> *Get-Process |*
>
> *where {($_.handles -gt 500)*
>
> *--or ($_.pm -ne 0)}*

Now that you took that other code and changed it out for the *-or* operator, the system will provide you with a different result than what you got the first time. This is the operator that you want to go with if you want to expand the amount of information that you are receiving. With this one, if the file or the document matches either one or both of the conditions, it will show up on your screen.

Since the document or file only needs to match up with one of the conditions rather than both of them, you end up with a lot of information to show up. It doesn't matter whether they meet both of these conditions or not, as long as they meet at least one of the conditions, they will pass inspection.

Now, let's look at this a bit further and see what will happen if you can add together the *-and* operator and the *-not* logical operator. Let's take a look at the code first:

> *Get-Process |*
>
> *where {($_.handles -gt 100)*
>
> *-and -not($_.company -eq*
>
> *"Microsoft Corporation")}*

With this example, we are telling the program that we do not want the handle to count up anything that is bigger than 100. We are also telling it that we are looking for a company name, but the answer can't be Microsoft Corporation. This line of code will go through and return illustrations that are not related to the Microsoft name.

Arithmetic operators

You will probably recognize a lot of the operators that are listed under this category. If you have done some form of math in the past, and you probably have, these will look pretty familiar to you. With the PowerShell language, you can work with some mathematical operations to get the code to work the way that you would like. You simply need to make sure that these can all go together and that it will make sense for the code that you are writing. Some of the arithmetic operators that you can work with are the following:

- (+)

This will add two values together.

- (-)

This one subtracts one value from another.

- (~)

This takes a value and converts it into a negative number.

- (*)

This one multiplies two values together.

- (/)

This divides two values.

- (%)

This one returns the remainder of numbers that you divided.

The arithmetic operators are some of the easiest ones that you can learn about in the PowerShell language. You can use them to add things together, to link strings of text together, and so much more.

Working with these operators adds a lot of functionality to the code that you are writing in PowerShell. You get to compare things, find ways to look up information on your computer, and so much more. Make sure to check out some of the operators and learn what they mean so that you can use them in your own code.

Chapter 5

Working with Strings and Quotes in PowerShell

There are a variety of syntaxes that you can work with when you are using PowerShell to make a code. The majority of these syntaxes add in some kind of string value. These are passed over to the commands as an argument. You will see that the strings are sometimes enclosed in a single quote, but you can work with a double quote as well. This chapter will focus on strings because it is important to know how they will work inside of your code.

String values

When you are writing your code, any time that you add in some quotes around the text that you are writing, no matter what you are writing, PowerShell is set up to see it like a string value. With this in mind, as long as the text does not add in any special characters or uses 'scalers,' you can choose whether or not that text is surrounded by double or single quotes. Special characters all have some different rules, but we will discuss that later.

When you are working with regular strings, the single and the double quotes both end up meaning the same thing. The important part is that your text should not have any special characters in it. It also matters that you start and stop the quotes the same way. It will not work if you start the string with single quotes and then end it with double quotes. We will take a look at two examples below. Even though they look a bit different, they both mean the same thing in PowerShell:

Write-Output "String in quotes."

Write-Output 'String in quotes.'

Also, there are times when you might want to use a quote within your string. This will work a bit differently than before. You have the freedom to choose if you want to put a single quote within a double quote or a double quote in a single quote like the following:

Write-Output "String 'in' quotes."

Write-Output 'String "in" quotes.'

If you mix these around and do it the other way, such as having a double inside a double with the quotes, you will find that the system will not read it the same way. Here are two examples of what you should avoid doing when it comes to adding a quote within a quote.

Write-Output "String "in" quotes."

Write-Output 'String 'in' quotes.'

If you decide to type both options into your PowerShell system, you will find that they are interpreted in different ways. With the last two illustrations that we wrote, you will see that in this return the quotes will not be displayed and there is a new line that will show up. This will happen since PowerShell interprets that one string is actually multiple strings and this ends with a line break.

Whenever you add some quotes to your code, you must make sure that you are writing the quotes the proper way. It is a good idea to always check these to make sure that they all match up and that you are not missing out on anything. If you forget to do this or if you have one that's missing a vital component, you could end up with a loop that will not end, depending on where you made the mistake. With this situation, the loop will be stuck, and it will keep asking for an entry, no matter what kind of answer you place inside.

If you are working on the program and you miss out on a quote, you may end up with a loop that keeps going on, and you will have to go back to the command prompt to get it fixed. A quick way to do this is with Win + R, then type in *cmd* or *cmd.exe* and press enter, so you can go through and fix the mistake.

How to add in special characters

With the examples that we have been talking about so far, you can choose which type of quote you would like to use. In those examples, you can work with either one because they basically mean the same thing. You just have to make sure that you used the same type of quote at the beginning as well as at the end of your string.

In some cases, what you chose will matter. There is a distinction that comes up with the double and the single quote. The single quote is the one that handles the string literally while the double quote will help you to escape any special characters that show up.

When the special character is preceded by the '`' or the 'backtick,' it takes on a specific action that cannot be accomplished without these symbols in place. Some of the special characters that you may need to use when you are working in PowerShell are:

- `0

This will insert a value that is null.

- `a

This will send an alert (which can be in the sound of a beep or a bell) to the speakers of your computer.

- `b

This one inserts a backspace.

- `f

This one inserts a form feed.

- `n

This one will insert a new line for you to use with the text.

- `r

This will insert a carriage return.

- `t

This will insert a horizontal tab.

- `v

This inserts a vertical.

- `'

This inserts a single quote.

- `"

This inserts a double quote.

One of the best ways to see how this concept works is to put into action. The illustration below is one with a few characters that have escaped. This is done so that you can see how the text will be displayed on your console:

Write-Output ("`n `tText includes: + `

"`n `t" escaped`" characters. `n")

The first character that will escape this illustration is the 'n.' Then the next one is the 'I' which will end up with the *ab* being inserted into your writing. Notice that the backtick that we used at the first line is not the escape character, but it can be used to show that your illustration will continue on. The double quotes will then show up around the escaped character, and they will then have a backtick ahead of them so that you can get the double quotes to show up at the output as well.

If you spent time trying to escape these characters even though they were within a string that was enclosed with just a single quote, then the backticks and the special characters won't show up on the output. This is because the single quotes will handle all the information literally. So, if we went with the single quotes rather than the double quotes, you will use the following syntax:

Write-Output '`tindented `n `twords'

If you take the time to place this on the console, you will just get the same thing to show up on the console because these strings only take the literal meaning. This is something that you should take note of because, in some of the older versions of PowerShell, you were allowed to do this with the single quotes, but this is something that was changed in the newer versions so make sure you use the right quotes.

System_String object members

Any time that you work with strings inside of PowerShell, it is important that they are handled in the same way that the *System_String* objects are. This is a good thing because it provides you with a ton of extra methods and properties that you can work with. As we spent some time talking about earlier, the 'Get-Member' command is used here to help you to retrieve the members of an object as they are pushed through the pipeline that you created. Since the string also passed just like with what happened to the objects, you can use the same command with the string. A good example of how this will work is the following:

"test output" | Get-Member

When you add this into your compiler, you can see that the string can support at least a few methods. These methods could include options like 'GetType' and 'Substring.' You can also go and scroll through the information a bit to find out the length property, which will let you know how many characters are already present in that string.

Let's take a look at how this could work. For this one, ay that we want to take a look at the Substring method and we would like to use your Get-Member command like we talked about above to help you to get the information. a good example of making this works includes the following illustration:

> *"test output"* |
>
> *Get-Member Substring* |
>
> *Format-List*

After you go through and run this illustration, you will observe that there are details which indicate how to utilize this method properly. There are also two styles of approach that you can use when you call this method. They include:

> *System.String Substring(Int32 startIndex)*
>
> *System.String Substring(Int32 start Index, Int32 length)*

In the first option, you provided the target string as well as an integer. This integer is used to specify the position from where you want the substring to start. This will cause the substring to have a return that starts in the right position and then it will continue on until it reaches the end of the string. This makes it easier if you would like to look at the whole string but want to start from a certain location. So, for what we are talking about, if you chose to go with the first option, you could type out something like the following:

> *("test output").Substring(5).*

This is a good one to work with because it allows you to have the test output come up and then it will start with the position of five on your substring. Remember that you can place just about any number that you would like here to make sure that the program starts right where you need it to. Of course, you have to make sure that you are putting the 'test output' in parentheses and that your period will come right after the method name so that it all works.

With the example that you worked with above, there are two methods that you can use. So, now it is time to take a look at how that second one will work. With that second one, you will provide the target string and the substring's starting length and point. If you want to make sure that you will start at a specific spot on the string, and you only want to let the program read a few lines of it, the second method is the one that would work the best for you. A good syntax that you could use is this:

("test output).Substring(0,4)

With that syntax, you can look at your output, which will start at the beginning since you used 0, which is considered the starting position. It is also set up to go over four characters. It is also possible to change the numbers and get them to do the number of characters and the starting point that works the best for you.

As you can see, there is a lot of power that comes into working with the PowerShell system. You can use some of the information that is found in this guidebook to make it easier to work with some of the codes that you want to write.

Chapter 6

The Drives and Providers

As you are working with PowerShell, there are many different files and folders that you can choose from. But first, you must make sure that you are providing the system with the right path name. The pathname usually starts with the simple C:\ and then it is followed by the remainder of the name that comes with the file or the folder that you want to work with. Any time that you would like to find a specific file system, you should double check that PowerShell needs to get the right name of the drive so that you can bring it up without too many issues.

Another thing that you will like is that some drives are not on your computer or on the file system driver but are supported by PowerShell so that you can get more storage and information to complete various tasks. A good example of this is the 'scaler' drive. The scaler drive helps you get ahold of the built-in scalers that you can work with on PowerShell. Let's take a quick look at some of the other drives that you can use with PowerShell and how you will be able to access them.

The PowerShell Providers

One more thing to keep in mind is that you need to work with a core which can be found in the data store inside of the PowerShell provider. One provider that you can work with is the Microsoft .NET and this layer shows up between the PowerShell and the data that you need to make sure that you can connect to the data stores through this service. For example, you can use your 'Get-Children' command to access a lot of information including the registry, certificate data stores, and file systems.

Many providers are already built into this program. If you want to have a look at the complete list of all these providers, you could just write out the command 'Get-PSProvider | select Name.' Some of the great providers that you can find inside of PowerShell include the following:

- **Alias**

These are the aliases that you can use to call the various commands that you want to use inside of PowerShell.

- **Certificate**

This is a process through Windows that is for digital signature certificates.

- **Environment**

This is a Windows environment scaler.

- **FileSystem**

This is the Windows file system drives, files, and folders.

- **Function**

These are the PowerShell functions.

- **Registry**

This is the Windows registry.

- **Scaler**

These are all the PowerShell scalers that we talked about earlier in this guidebook.

As you look through this list, it is easy to see that some of the processes are available with the help of the Windows programming, which shows how well these two programs work together. And when they do come together, you can get all the benefits of both at the same time. These providers are important because they are a huge part of the coding process, but you will not see them inside of PowerShell all that often. This is because you are more likely to see the drives that are inside your system, and these will help you to access the provider even if you don't need to see it.

What are the built-in drives?

The first thing that we will have to do here is to take some time to look at the PowerShell drives that are found automatically inside the PowerShell system. These drives are utilized on a regular basis to return data from your providers. Basically, the file system data is exposed to the PowerShell drive that corresponds to that Windows drive. The C drive will then be able to access the data by a file system which will then expose the Windows C drive to the system. A good example of the code that you can use to make all of this happen looks like the following:

Get-PSDrive | sort Provider, Name

With that illustration above, you can sort it by the provider first and then you will receive the name. This will make the sorting a bit easier because all of the providers are grouped in together, and then you can take a look from there to see how many drives each provider can hold. In the illustration above, you will also see that the root information you can use to help you locate the target data store is also displayed.

If you are taking a look at this and you would like to get more information on the drives, you would just need to use the Get-PSDrive command and then type in the information that you are looking for to make it work. So, if you are trying to format a list, you could type out the command 'Get-PSDrive Function | Format List', and it would all be done.

How to create your own drive

While there are a ton of drives that you can choose from when you use PowerShell there are times when you might feel those drives are not exactly what you would like for your program. This is usually when you want to create a new drive on the system. These are drives that are based at least a little bit on the providers that already exist on your PowerShell, which means that the process is a bit easier to handle. But, you can use this information to make something that is completely new.

Let's try making a new drive for PowerShell. First, you need to use the New-PSDrive command like you did before. Let's take a look at an example of a syntax that we would use while working on the drive named *ps*.

New-PSDrive -Name ps

-PSProvider FileSystem -Root $pshome

With the illustration that we just worked on above, you will notice that it will take some time to identify the name that you would like to call the new drive with, and it will keep going so that you can name both the provider and the root. When you run this particular illustration, PowerShell knows that it needs to create a new drive. Once it is done, PowerShell will display the information that you need, so you see what is on the drive.

At this point, you will notice that any information that shows up always include the root name, rather than the traditional scaler name. After you finish writing out the new drive and creating it, you can use it in the exact same manner that you would use the built-in drives. You just need to make sure that the locale is changed for operating that new drive, and you can do this with the following syntax:

*cd ps: *

There are also times when you have to remove or delete a drive that you created or defined, and you just need to use the 'Remove-PSDrive' command. It is important to keep track of the drives that you are in because you can't delete a drive that you are currently working on. So, once you change the operating locale, you can use the following illustration to remove that drive:

cd C:\; Remove-PSDrive ps.

As you are working on this, it is important to remember that when you create a new drive, it will only stay valid during the session that it was created. This is helpful because you don't need to go through it after you are done with the program and delete or otherwise remove drives or processors unless there is some other reason for doing this because they will automatically do this when you close it out. It can be a hassle if you are working on several systems that need the same new drives, but it does not take long to create these at all.

Creating these new drives will help you to determine where you will work inside the PowerShell system. You get the choice of creating your own or using one that is already a part of the program. Use the steps above to help create a device of your own so that you can get the hang of this and learn how to make it work for your own coding needs.

Conclusion

Thank you for making it through to the end of this book, let's hope it was informative and that it was able to provide you with all of the tools you need to achieve your goals whatever they may be.

The next step is to decide when you are ready to start working in PowerShell. There are so many cool things that you can do once you learn this programming language and with the help of the powerful Windows system, it will work out for you in no time. If you feel like you are ready to start learning more about PowerShell, make sure to check out this guidebook today!

Finally, if you found this book useful in any way, a review on Amazon is always appreciated!

PowerShell

The Utmost Intermediate Course Guide in Fundamentals and Concept of PowerShell Programming

Introduction to PowerShell

Congratulations on purchasing *PowerShell: The Utmost Intermediate Course Guide in Fundamentals and Concept of PowerShell Programming a*nd thank you for doing so. There are plenty of books on this subject on the market, thanks again for choosing this one! Every effort was made to ensure it is full of as much useful information as possible, please enjoy!

The following chapters discuss scripting using Microsoft PowerShell. There are many tools available for integrating automation into your Windows environment. Today's administrators need flexible and highly extensible options to fit the multitude of tasks necessary. PowerShell is different than BASH or VBScript because it takes detailed and complex scripts and condenses them into highly flexible tools available not just for personal use, but also for packaging so any administrator can take advantage of them even if they are not a scripting expert.

The purpose of PowerShell is to make an administrator's life easier. Windows is a Graphical User Interface (GUI), and although that makes using it much more accessible, it also limits its flexibility. The only way to perform operations more quickly using the standard GUI interface is to point, click and type faster. On the other hand, PowerShell enables you to perform a given task on hundreds or thousands of machines simultaneously. All administrators are not the same. If two users are performing the same task, given all things being equal, and one user performs the function in seconds while the other takes minutes, it's pretty clear which administrator would be the more effective one. That is the beauty of PowerShell! An administrator who knows PowerShell only performs many tasks a single time, and after that initial configuration, every time that same operation appears they can perform it at the click of a button instead of traversing the GUI or writing out repetitive scripts every time they need to manage a system. In short, PowerShell isn't just a handy tool for an administrator's tool belt; it's a hammer, it's a saw. It is one of the essential tools for any administrator operating in a Windows environment.

Chapter 1

A Brief History of Scripting

Introduced in the first version of Unix in 1971, and written by Ken Thompson, Thompson Shell was a simple command interpreter. It was not designed for scripting but introduced several features to the command-line interface. You cannot talk about scripting or shell programs at all without talking about Ken Thompson and his peers working for Bell Labs in the 1970's. Bell Labs hired Thompson in 1966, and initially, he worked on Multics, an operating system developed at MIT in coordination with Bell Labs and General Electric. Out of necessity since Bell Labs decided not to continue the Multics partner project, Thompson wrote some tools that later developed into UNIX because of his desire to play a video game that he wrote while working on Multics.

While working on UNIX, it quickly became apparent to Thompson that his new file system needed a programming language. He and Dennis Ritchie co-authored B language which is the precursor to the C programming language. Not only did Ken Thompson develop Unix and its first system programming language, but he also is responsible for the creation of the concept of computer processes and device files. In Windows, a device is anything that interfaces with a device driver, while in Unix these are called device files because they appear in the file system as regular files.

However, as time passed the functionality of Thompson's Shell program in Unix became insufficient for the programming needs of Bell Labs, and thus others at Bell began to modify Thompson's shell to accommodate the needs of their team. This transition to a desire for the shell program to accommodate the needs of programmers was evident in v6.0 of Unix. Version 7.0 is where Unix matures into a more refined application which now includes the replacement for Thompson's Shell, called Bourne Shell, named after its creator Stephen Bourne also of Bell Labs. The Bourne Shell or "/sh" is still in current day Unix systems of all kinds. There have been numerous features added since its inception in 1979, and a complete revamp called Bourne-Again Shell or "/bash" which was designed to be more user-friendly with features such as auto-complete and numerous other quality of life enhancements for the power-user.

Microsoft developed PowerShell, but why did they feel the need to include high-level script programming in Windows above and beyond what they had always been using, batch files, command files and VBScript to execute scripts useful for programmers and administrators? A complete answer to that question could be a whole different book, but if you look at PowerShell, it is very similar to Unix shells because of its flexibility. Most importantly I think Microsoft recognized the power of being able to unify the control and administration of their complete software lineup through a single interface. Microsoft's development of its current lineup of GUI interface software is already performing PowerShell commands behind the scenes, and this includes Sharepoint, Exchange Server, Systems Center products, Office 365 and even Windows itself. Regarding Microsoft's goals, it is clear to see that PowerShell is necessary for anyone who works in a Microsoft environment whether it is for programming, systems administration, desktop support or database administration because of this connection to PowerShell. Administrators and power-users at all levels can benefit from this robust tool capable of interfacing with nearly all aspects of a Windows Enterprise environment.

Before PowerShell, Windows used batch files for scripting, but the scripting language was rudimentary, and the functionality limited due to a lack of command line equivalency between batch files and command line operations. Other prior attempts to integrate scripting such as Window Script Host also failed for various reasons ranging from lack of documentation to issues related to system security. Microsoft Windows as a platform was left behind regarding its ability to support extensive automation and administration compared to the functionality available to Unix based environments. As an organization, they understood that this was something that had to change if maintaining their market dominance is a priority. Internally at Microsoft, some of the leadership wanted to use Unix tools to manage Windows because of its flexibility. There are critical differences in the architecture of Unix vs. Windows, and due to these differences, the ability to effectively communicate with Windows API's using Unix tools was cumbersome and ultimately ineffective. The turning point for scripting in the Windows environment happened when Windows PowerShell officially released in 2006, but work began behind the scenes a few years prior. Struggling unsuccessfully to integrate Unix tools into Windows turned Microsoft on the path to developing a new solution. Microsoft Shell (known internally as Monad) began development around 2002 and was brought out for demonstration at the PDC conference in late 2003. A series of beta tests began, and two years later they released their Monad beta shell to the public. In the following year, the final phases of development completed, and Microsoft renamed Monad to Windows PowerShell. The name Windows PowerShell was important because Microsoft wanted its user base to know that this product was intended to be a central feature of Windows and not just another one of many software offerings.

Microsoft has always stood out from the rest of the computing world for its insistence on closed-source applications, whereas Unix always enjoyed a much more extensive development community because there are no barriers to obtaining the software. The development of PowerShell remained internal for nearly a decade, but eventually, Microsoft decided that to continue improving PowerShell and allowing it to grow according to the needs of the users it needed to be set free and indeed, set free it was. In 2016 Microsoft announced that PowerShell, no longer Windows PowerShell would be open-source and available on platforms and environments other than Windows. Microsoft has a long history with a strategy of embracing and extending to open source organizations to extinguish their market influence or use their massive financial influence to stifle any potential threats. However, this one hundred and eighty degree turn around is a significant change in ideology for Microsoft. Microsoft's profitability is shifting to services, servers and cloud computing (Azure) which are run on Unix based systems. With this change in ideology comes a new relationship with the open-source market. The leadership in Redmond, WA at the headquarters realizes that demanding their customers use only Windows branded products throughout their entire environment was no longer realistic. Even inside Microsoft's own environment, they no longer run a one hundred percent Windows architecture, because it simply no longer made sense from a business perspective.

Today, we are witness to the advent of a new era not just for Microsoft but computing as a whole. There are innumerable options in the technology sector, but Windows and Linux are the two most significant and most recognizable, and for the entirety of the history of both of these platforms they have been fundamentally opposing forces to one another. One is open, and the other closed, one is about empowerment and the other control. This philosophical difference is no more. Today, these two giants of the technology world are finally moving in the same direction. The best part about this shifting ideology is that the change is most directly going to benefit the customer, it provides more options for systems architects when designing because the need for applications that tie systems together is lessened or eliminated entirely.

Chapter 2

Executing Commands

PowerShell isn't only scripting; it's also about running commands. Scripting entails entering keywords into a text editor, saving the script and then running the script to test it. Executing commands is more active, Commands are entered into the shell, administrators modify those commands for the desired effect and then execute. In return, PowerShell runs those commands to immediate impact. Continually using PowerShell teaches users to learn to take those same commands and enter them into a text editor and save them with the .ps1 file extension and voilà you now have a PowerShell script. Whatever commands are run often enough to copy down into a script, are easily automated. No more typing to get the desired result, now running that command is merely a matter of double-clicking the script file. So what exactly is a command in PowerShell? Microsoft calls PowerShell commands, cmdlets (pronounced command-lets). The correct syntax is imperative when running cmdlets, but in the most basic form, a PowerShell command is formatted verb-noun, such as Get-Process.

The cmdlet naming convention

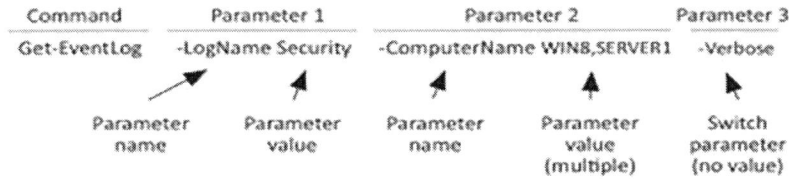

In the above example, the cmdlet Get-EventLog is run.

An investigation of the structure of this command is needed. First, take notice of the command to the far left and then the parameters that define what EventLog will be retrieved. The first parameter is -LogName Security, which says we want to view the security log. The second parameter is "-computername", which means we want to display the security log on a specific computer. The third parameter -Verbose says, show the full information available. Verbose is a switch command and does not need any further definition. The dictionary defines verbose as "using or expressed in more words than needed" this is common in scripting and programming to tell a program to return complete information to the user.

There are also some critical formatting tips to keep in mind when entering cmdlets. Do not include spaces between the dash and the text, parameters always begin with a dash, ensure that a space is placed between parameters. These are the most basic of basics regarding cmdlets in PowerShell.

It is vital to understand these basics though because they will become a foundation for increasingly complex iterations that will make your work faster and shorter once you learn to navigate through them. There are myriad ways to expand upon cmdlets, but two of the most common are aliases and truncation. An alias is a shortened version of a cmdlet, for example, Tom runs the *Get-Service* command dozens of times a day, and after tiring of typing the full cmdlet out every single time, he decides to check the help section seeking an alias for *Get-Service*.

He discovers that "gsv" is the system defined alias for *Get-Service*. I say system defined alias because custom user-defined aliases are also possible but that is something that this book does not cover. Truncation works a bit differently than aliases; instead of looking for a shorter string of characters to perform the same action, truncation acts as an on-demand wildcard to auto-complete whatever character string is entered. If Tom wanted to use the "-computername" cmdlet he could type "-compu" and with a tab keystroke, PowerShell will search its known database of cmdlets and bring up a single match. The single match part is also critical because for truncation to function, you have to type enough of the name for PowerShell to be able to distinguish it from other possibilities. It is also possible to replace parameters not just cmdlets with aliases, and this is something to keep in mind as your skill with PowerShell develops.

The help command is the most effective method of expanding usable knowledge of PowerShell. Mastering PowerShell to use it from day one effectively is not required. Aliases for cmdlets and parameters are found using the help function. The next level of self-learning is the *Show-Command* cmdlet which attempts to handle the parameters of any given command and completes the syntax for you. Tom wants to find an event log located on a remote machine, but every time he runs the command, red text is returned to him displaying a syntax error. Tom can use the *Show-Command* cmdlet and PowerShell will prompt him graphically for the cmdlet and the parameters he would like to apply. This feature isn't in every version of PowerShell, but it comes with all versions after v3.0.

We've discussed how to format cmdlets and how to modify them using alias, truncation and other neat tips that will make your PowerShell life easier but one of the most critical aspects of PowerShell is the actual interface. There are two ways of interacting with PowerShell, one being the console and the other being the integrated scripting environment or ISE. The differences are seemingly minor at first, but those small differences add up to make one version superior in almost every way. The console is purely a command-line interface, and so it is always available, even on devices that do not have a graphical interface such as some kinds of servers. The ISE, on the other hand, requires a GUI available and it displays much more information about the console operations than the standalone console does. The ISE includes a list of commands on the right-hand side of the window and a scripting pane right above the console pane, and because it's a GUI interface it also is empowered with lots of tool-tips and other user-friendly and generally informative features that simplify the brainpower needed to understand data displayed. In the next section, we will discuss how to use the help system to uncover and educate yourself on the minutiae of PowerShell.

One of Microsoft's own scripting MVP's declared "If you aren't willing to read PowerShell's help files, you won't be effective with PowerShell. You won't learn how to use it, you won't learn how to administer products like Windows with it, and you might as well stick with the GUI." This quote is sage advice and if this book intends to assist its reader then I would be remiss not discussing the help system.

Using the help system is critical for expanding usable knowledge of the inner working of PowerShell. The developers created the help section with the expectation that it would be the primary knowledge resource for users wanting to learn PowerShell. Locating unknown commands to perform a given operation requires using the help system to find the command. Running commands that return an error require using the help system to reveal the proper syntax so that syntax errors do not impede your task. Piping multiple commands together to perform a complex task requires the help system to learn how each command connects to the next one.

Everyone using computers gets accustomed to searching the internet for answers to questions, but in this case, you do not need to search the internet; the most efficient way to proceed is to learn how to use the help command so that you can create solutions independently. Every little detail is not in the help file, and a lot of the highly-advanced topics also are not documented there, but in regards to being a productive day-to-day administrator, it is positively imperative to master the help system.

PowerShell has a cmdlet, *Get-Help*, that accesses the help system. *Get-Help* has several parameters. One of those parameters "-Name" specifies the name of the help topic you would like to access, and it is a positional parameter, so you do not have to type "-Name"; just provide the name of the cmdlet. It also accepts wildcards, which make the help system useful for discovering commands. Tom would enter *Get-Help event* to display a list of every command that has the word event in it, even if that command was not directly related to what he was seeking.

PowerShell's help system also includes background topics, in addition, to provide help for specific cmdlets. These background topics are often called about topics because their filenames all start with the word about. There are the common parameters that all cmdlets support, and if you type help *common* you should see a help item titled *about_common_parameters*. Another often overlooked tip is to type help *about* to retrieve all of the about files in the help system. This additional documentation reveals a surprising amount of depth behind cmdlets outside of syntax concerns. Essential information to impart to readers is to mention the necessity of the *Update-Help* cmdlet. When you first access PowerShell, the help file is not pre-packaged.

You cannot access any of the sage advice in the help systems about files or anything regarding cmdlets at all until you run this command. Running *Update-Help* should be the very first operation you perform when you launch the PowerShell console. In this same vein, depending on what version of Windows you are running, you likely do not have the latest version of PowerShell available. The capabilities of PowerShell expand in each iteration, usually. Microsoft has links to where you can find the latest version of PowerShell on Microsoft.com and using the current version is recommended.

Chapter 3

Provider Essentials

One of the more confusing aspects of PowerShell is its use of Providers. It is likely that some familiarity with Window's filesystem and maybe even commands to manage it from the command line tool, cmd.exe are present already. Harnessing that prior understanding to clarify what a provider is and why it is vital to understanding how PowerShell operates is the goal of this chapter.

A PowerShell provider, or PSProvider, is an adapter. It is designed to take a data store and make it look like a disk drive. PSProviders allow an administrator to work with different data containers all within a single interface. Entering the command *Get-PSProvider* lets PowerShell return a list of possible repositories. Thinking in terms of the Windows command line, a user might change directories with the switch "cd" or create directories with "md," but attempts to create new entries in the registry would not make sense, it simply is not a part of the functionality of cmd.exe. PowerShell has no such limitations though, and it is capable of creating new directories in the filesystem or creating new entries in the registry through the power of Providers.

The concept of providers can occasionally be confusing, but PowerShell's ability to do many things while simultaneously interacting with many containers is possible because of this process. Providers are used for creating PSDrives, and PSDrive is a location to a data repository managed by software called a Provider. It is very similar to creating a drive mapping, as you would in Windows Explorer, but a PSDrive can connect to many different types of resources. The Provider translates the actions of cmdlets into something the PSDrive understands.

Tom wants to see all the subfolders in his C: drive, so he should type *Get-ChildItem*, this cmdlet will function whether he is looking in the filesystem or the registry because the Provider translates the differences in file structure for the user automatically. There are many different providers available depending on which modules you use, but some common ones are registry, functions, the certificate store, and the file system.

The hierarchical structure of the Windows filesystem contains three main types of objects: drives, folders, and files. Drives are at the top, then folders and lastly files. PowerShell doesn't use this same terminology because it isn't always operating on the file system, it could be performing actions on an Environment or modifying the way a Function performs, and because of these varied needs, users need terminology that fits all of these situations.

The most confusing aspect of Providers is understanding what capabilities the provider is allowing. One example might be attempting to use the -itemproperties parameter while inside an Environment PSDrive. The Provider knows to structure the Environmental data hierarchically, but these environmental variables do not have item properties. They are item properties themselves, so the "-itemproperties" parameter does not make sense, it won't work. There is a great deal of depth on the subject of Providers, but for our purposes, the most crucial aspect is knowing that they exist.

Chapter 4

Custom & External Commands

In chapter two, we discussed how to use the help system to expand independent learning. A significant component of that learning includes discovering how to manage with error messages. It is practically inevitable that at some point while using PowerShell, commands that do not work correctly will consume your attention. PowerShell communicates this by displaying an error message in red text, to grab your attention. Errors in syntax already have a tool called *Show-Command* that helps you understand where syntax errors occur. These red error messages can be disconcerting, but they also attempt to be helpful. Examining the red text closely, points out where PowerShell encountered an issue with the previous instruction. Error messages usually include the line and character number where PowerShell did not understand the previous instruction.

In the above example, PowerShell is saying, "Get was entered, what does that mean?" That is because the wrong command name was entered. The correct command name is *Get-Command*, not the hyphen-less Get Command.

PowerShell is an incredibly powerful tool, and one of the most flexible options that it supports is the creation of custom commands. In other words, you can create custom cmdlets that allow for functions that are not pre-programmed into the shell. The idea behind this functionality is to enable programmers to create custom behaviors to support or enhance their programming scripts. Creating cmdlets can be an extensive operation but creating a simple cmdlet begins with creating a verb-noun combination that can be used to invoke the new cmdlet.

Microsoft's own MSDN website hosts some valuable examples and even tutorials on creating custom commands. Custom Commands can support the full capabilities of PowerShell, including declaration parameters or sets of parameters, dynamic parameters, invoking scripts from within a cmdlet, parameter validation, support for transactions and jobs, ShouldProcess calls and even calling a separate cmdlet from within a custom cmdlet. Custom commands can be a compelling option for enterprise operations that require custom application support and extensive automation support.

Creating custom commands allow corporations to internally develop the tools necessary to properly manage a given environment instead of outsourcing the creation and management of functions and applications that require automated support. Instead of outsourcing direct support, a small portion of the cost of an outsourced solution could be re-directed to the internal development of automated support solutions. In today's corporate landscape many corporations are now choosing automation over human interaction because of the short-term cost savings. There is potential for long-term cost savings as well, for solutions that are developed in a customer-centric fashion, however not all systems are created equal. That is a subject for a different book though.

Some critical parameters to consider when creating a custom command are the *Set-Alias* cmdlet which creates or changes an alias for a given cmdlet, *Get-Verb*, which displays a list of approved verbs to assign to the new cmdlet. Consistency is crucial in the implementation of cmdlets, and these approved verbs allow cmdlet creators to select words that maintain that consistency. Microsoft has a set of standards that would be considered "Best Practices" when creating cmdlets.

Every cmdlet must have parameters for the command to follow, setting those parameters should be based on the intended effect of the script or functionality. Once a script and associated parameters are created what process takes it to the next level? The answer is simple, increase the flexibility of the script to create an advanced function. A simple script is used to perform a single function. An advanced function performs the same action as the simple script but caters to the usability of many potential users. Imagine a script that is used to create new users in Active Directory, but only a single administrator uses the script.

The script is executed when receiving the new hires list every month from HR. Taking this script and turning it into an advanced function would mean that I have placed the script in a central location such as a network drive, then defined the script in PowerShell by creating a .ps1 file that adds a Verb-Noun relationship defining the create new user script. Then the next step is to polish the advanced function by converting all of the parameter inputs in the original script, to allow the input of arrays of data. All this means is that more than a single data point is eligible to be filled in where our parameters are.

Creating data arrays, even if they are a singular data point, allows the custom cmdlet to be piped into another cmdlet the same as every native cmdlet allows. Once the parameters can accept an array of data, the next step is binding the parameters to the custom cmdlet. Parameters that are available to all cmdlets by default are now available to the newly created custom cmdlet as well. At this point, we now have a functioning cmdlet, but there is still a myriad of options to decide on; for instance, does your custom cmdlet require any parameters to execute correctly?

In the case of our new hire script, yes! We at least need at least one unique identifier such as a name or employee number before the command can process correctly. What is most important to understand, is that once the cmdlet is defined, we need to create support for PowerShell's built-in parameters. Once the custom cmdlet functions similarly to a native cmdlet, then it is ready to be deployed amongst clients.

Another important aspect of compatibility and system adoption includes being able to support the functionality that an existing user base is already accustomed to using. PowerShell does this as well through its ability to support external commands. What is an external command? External commands are cmdlets that are not native to the PowerShell installation. They come as separate modules packaged with Microsoft software such as Exchange, Sharepoint, SQL, but these applications are not the only sources of new external commands. It includes the use of older; built-in Windows features such as ipconfig, nslookup, set and many other commands.

Even old command line tools that are not native to Windows still function normally. If BASH were installed, all the tools and syntax that have grown comfortable by using that tool become available and PowerShell can display the results in the same manner that BASH always has displayed the results in. The vital information to remember is the fact that PowerShell does not force you to learn everything from scratch, if there are tools that are familiar, continue using them as you always have.

There are some caveats to this approach, as we discovered in our earlier discussion about Providers, PowerShell needs to translate the user input into something PowerShell can understand, and the parser does an excellent job at this, but no system is perfect and complex commands with multiple variables and arguments can cause problems. Luckily for us, older versions of PowerShell offer workaround solutions for these instances, but newer versions have added a much cleaner and simpler solution. Adding two dashes and a percentile sign before the command communicates to the shell that the following command should pass through without parsing.

Executing custom commands, external commands and resolving error messages are all a part of using PowerShell the way that YOU want to. Highly extensible, customizable solutions are exactly what every enterprise organization needs and to that end, there are a few more jewels of wisdom that may come in handy while learning PowerShell.

PowerShell allows for the use of profile scripts which can be used to customize the PowerShell environment, by loading modules, changing which directory the shell focuses on at launch, defining functions that you might use commonly, and so on.

Profiles allow for each user to customize his or her console installation to match their particular preferences as individuals. Profiles are a good idea for administrators who may share a workstation or work form many different physical locations. Please reference the help entry, *about_profiles* for more detailed information about how to setup and execute a profile. Other ways that the shell can be customized include, customizing the colors used and modifying the syntax of the prompt, which by default is PS C:\.

Chapter 5

Snap-Ins, Modules and adding new tools to PowerShell

PowerShell has two kinds of extensions: modules and snap-ins. PowerShell snap-ins are referenced as PSSnapin, which distinguishes them from snap-ins for the graphical MMC (Microsoft Management Console). A PSSnap-in contains DLL files and usually XML files that contain configuration settings and help text pertinent to the toolkit. PSSnap-ins have to be installed and registered for PowerShell to recognize their presence. Microsoft designed PowerShell along similar lines to the Microsoft Management Console, and in fact, the same team that is responsible for developing the MMC is also responsible for the design implementation of PowerShell.

MMC is a ubiquitous tool for managing various aspects of the Windows environment and commonly, administrators snap-in the Remote Server Administration Tools to access Active Directory Users and Computers. Being familiar with the MMC helps to understand the design philosophy behind PowerShell itself. When you launch PowerShell, it only loads the default modules, however, similar to MMC there are a plethora of available snap-ins regarding other Microsoft products that the shell can register. The strength of snap-ins is the flexibility that they allow. PowerShell can only do so much on its own, it relies heavily on installed snap-ins and modules, but when you set up an environment equipped with the proper tools, the functionality of the toolkit is incredible.

The concept of fitting snap-ins for PowerShell is vital to understand because they are still a part of PowerShell but the direction of creating additional utilities is shifting more towards Modules. Snap-ins registered into Window Registry are written in a .NET language and must be available as an assembly. Microsoft's definition of an Assembly is, "a collection of resources and types that are built to work together and create a unit of logical functionality." Assembled solutions take more effort to create and to manage and require executable installation files to add their functionality to PowerShell. These downsides have shifted the focus to modules as they are more flexible, extensible and more manageable.

Modules contained in a folder are loaded automatically as long as PowerShell is aware of the file path. There is a default path for modules, and any modules available at the startup of PowerShell are stored in this default path folder. Modules are designed to be self-contained and more straightforward to distribute. A note worth mentioning, PowerShell v1.0 is snap-in focused and in v2.0 the focus shifts to modules, but these modules require a declaration in the console host to load. After PowerShell 2.0, the shell automatically performs this operation, and since PowerShell is open-source now, take the time to install the most current version.

The environment variable "PSModulePath" defines the location where PowerShell looks for modules to load; also, it is not definable from within PowerShell. It is a part of the Windows environment, to change it, modify the parameter within the System Control Panel, or configure it via Group Policy. The actual path is critical because more current versions of PowerShell are capable of auto-discovering modules and even loading on demand, including help files for commands located within specific modules without any new cmdlets, other than *Update-Help*.

Modules contain new cmdlets for PowerShell as previously discussed, but how does PowerShell differentiate between cmdlets with the same character string? When two cmdlets have identical text, executing that cmdlet creates a conflict. PowerShell runs the most recently loaded command, but that also makes it difficult to reach the other version of that command, likely referring to the contents of a separate module. It is accomplished by referencing the complete path of the first module loaded and entering the cmdlet name, but this requires unnecessary typing, and it also necessitates knowing where the module is stored at in the file system.

A cleaner and simpler solution is to add a prefix specific to the module. If overlap occurs with default or loaded modular commands, then creating prefixes prevents conflicts. It also is possible to remove the offending module entirely using *Remove-PSSnapin* or *Remove-Module*, along with the snap-in or the module name. Included below is a snapshot of the syntax and parameters directly from the help system for the *Get-Module* cmdlet. Quoted from the Help system as well, "Beginning in PowerShell 3.0, you can use the *Get-Module* cmdlet as well as *Import-Module* to retrieve and import Common Information Model (CIM) modules, in which the cmdlets defined are Cmdlet Definition XML (CDXML) files.

This feature allows you to use cmdlets that have implementations in non-managed code assemblies, such as those written in C++." The quote requires explanation, but it is saying *Get-Module*, as well as *Import-Module*, are cmdlets central to managing a heterogeneous enterprise environment that includes Windows as well as devices running other operating systems.

One of PowerShell's features includes user-defined variables. These variables allow quick access to pre-defined resources, such as objects, commands, output, computer names, files, processes, services or anything else. Variables are containers to place things in, add objects to, or retrieve items from. Even after retrieving the variable, the specified items stay in the container, allowing you to recover them repeatedly. Microsoft creates object-oriented applications, and because the base of everything is on that orientation, the flexibility of variables is limited only by the imagination of the shell's user. As stated, variables are flexible, but facets of variable definition require some caution. The following points are items to keep in mind when creating new variables. Variable names are comprised of letters, numbers, and underscores. Variable names can contain spaces, but {braces} are required. Microsoft recommends variable names that do not include spaces or special characters; also, variables do not persist between sessions, so when you close the shell any variables you defined terminate as well. Saving a variable for a future session is possible, add it to your PowerShell profile.

The available memory is the only limitation on the length of variable names, so employ variable names that are logical without being cumbersome to type. PowerShell allows variable name prefixes, but it is no longer considered a "Best Practices" technique. A Variable name prefix would be a prefix added to a variable, indicating what type of data the variable contains. Storing variables requires the proper syntax, informing PowerShell of an upcoming variable requires the dollar sign followed by the variable name. Variables substitutions replace parameter values, and PowerShell contains a feature regarding variable replacement that can be useful in some situations.

Generally, single quotations are used around text strings to signify literal interpretation, but double quotation marks instruct PowerShell to seek out dollar signs within quotes and replace any variables it finds with the contents of the variable container.

A single variable can contain multiple objects of different types. PowerShell references the individual objects after the user has defined an index number in [square] brackets. It is also possible to view the properties and methods of an object inside a variable. PowerShell v2.0 and earlier, this process required some clever manipulation via piping a variable to a cmdlet to enumerate it since you cannot reference the individual objects contained within the variable without declaring a bracketed [number] and then applying a method to view the properties.

The process required to view properties of variables was, and Microsoft developed a new process for all versions after v3.0 called automatic unrolling. The way automatic unrolling works is when you attempt to call the properties of a variable if the collection the variable is referencing does not contain the properties listed but items within the collection DO contain the properties declared then PowerShell knows to enumerate the objects within the collection automatically. Then it retrieves the property declared in the cmdlet returning the output.

The last point to make regarding adding functionality to the shell is regarding how to declare what type of data a variable contains explicitly. PowerShell manipulates data, but it is entirely up to the user to ensure that PowerShell understands precisely what kind of data manipulation is required to reach the desired result. Declaring the data type of a variable is how to make sure that PowerShell handles the data appropriately. The default way PowerShell processes variable data may not suit a given situation.

Declaring the type of information, the variable contains is done with square brackets input before the $ declaring the variable, preventing entry of incorrect data types and limiting the shell to a single type of data for the operation. The reason to declare the data type relates to possible misinterpretations of data. PowerShell treats everything as an object, because of this, numbers, dates, arrays, XML and other data types are misinterpreted even if the format is apparent to a human.

Entering a date with format x/x/xx does not necessarily mean that PowerShell can understand it is a date. It may read that as a string object and not understand how to parse the date to achieve the result the administrator is looking to achieve. Operations such as determining the amount of time, in days or hours from one date to another are simple calculations for a human, but the shell only understands how to calculate dates if you explicitly tell it that dates are the only data manipulation required for this operation.

Many other types of variable declarations exist, take the time to research on MSDN and run the cmdlet help *about_variables* to learn more. Variables are also related to scope, which is not discussed, but the help file provides some insights. In short, the scope is the level at which a defined variable is available for use.

Chapter 6

Fully Automatic: Using the Pipeline to connect commands and create powerful tools

There are many different choices when it comes to selecting a shell for scripting, but what makes PowerShell unique is not the way it runs commands, instead it is the way it allows multiple commands to be connected to each other in sequence. PowerShell connects commands to each other by using a pipeline. The pipeline provides a method for one command to send its output to the next command, allowing the second command in the pipeline to take the output of the first command and process it as parameters.

A common approach to using the pipeline is to compare sets of data using it. Running a cmdlet and piping the results to *Export-CliXML* or *Export-CSV* allows administrators the ability to review and analyze sets of data or share the data with others. PowerShell also comes equipped with the *Compare-Object* cmdlet, which allows for comparisons of data sets from directly within the shell. Use these techniques for taking baseline measurements of a system and then comparing future data against the baseline to create management reports.

Using the help system allows the discovery of variable output commands. Running a query on system processes using *Get-Process* displays a list of all processes running on the device, however, you could pipe those results into a file or send them to a printer or even discover other methods using *Help *out**. Using a pipe to connect a series of commands expand what is possible for an administrator to accomplish in a finite time. Using the cmdlets:

Get-Service | ConvertTo-HTML | Out-File services.html

constructs a document in HTML format of currently running services on a machine. Creating a document in this manner is an example of using three cmdlets piped together to create a document that is ready to be uploaded to the intranet in literally seconds. Crafting a document manually, listing active services is a time-consuming process, not even considering the time to format and upload the document. Each command handles a single step in the process and the entire command line as a whole accomplishes a task. The above example has little system impact as our cmdlet sequence is creating documentation; however, a different series of cmdlets could potentially crash or significantly impede the operation of a system, which takes us to our next topic regarding the impact of a given cmdlet.

All cmdlets that change the system in some way have a defined impact level. Cmdlets that can significantly change the computer are considered to have a high level of "Impact." PowerShell has an internal value for each cmdlet, regarding impact, and it uses an algorithm to determine the impact of piped cmdlets linked together. When a cmdlets internal impact level is equal to or higher than the shell's *$ConfirmPreference* setting(a pre-defined variable), the shell automatically prompts, "Are you sure?" It is also possible to tell the system to prompt you regardless of a cmdlet's impact by using the "-confirm" parameter.

A similar parameter, "-whatif" is supported by any cmdlet that supports the "-confirm" cmdlet, but the "-whatif" parameter does not automatically appear based on impact. "-Whatif" is important because it provides a way to preview what a potentially dangerous cmdlet would have done to the system. Logically, some commands are more useful when piped than others. It is possible to pair illogical commands together, but the effects are impossible, inert, or complete nonsense most often.

Stringing together two commands leaves PowerShell to determine how to get the output of the first command to the input of the second command, and this is the crux of the issue. PowerShell can only accept input on a parameter, so when piping one cmdlet to another, the shell determines which parameter of the first cmdlet is acceptable by the second cmdlet.

If the first cmdlet does not have acceptable parameters, then the pipeline parameter binding fails. Pipeline parameter binding is the process that PowerShell uses to determine if a set of cmdlets can agree. Understanding this relationship is the key to maximizing the effectiveness of PowerShell. An administrator could still be highly effective without a deep understanding of this aspect of the system, but it would require more time, more effort and more writing to do the same as an administrator who mastered piping commands. There are many essential aspects to understanding PowerShell, but this is the defining feature of the system, without this aspect we could merely use VBScript or a different shell to perform the same action.

PowerShell uses multiple methods to determine whether a set of cmdlets match. First, PowerShell looks at the type of object produced by the first cmdlet and tries to see whether any parameter of the second cmdlet can accept that type of object from the pipeline. Investigate this in the ISE console, by using *Get-Member* to determine what type of object the first cmdlet is producing. Armed with that knowledge we can look at the full help for the second cmdlet and see if it is, in fact, capable of accepting the output of the first cmdlet as a parameter.

Using this method of matching is slow at first, but with practice, it becomes easier to identify cmdlets that are suitable for piping to one another. Trial and error is always an option, but if accuracy is a priority then taking the time to confirm the pairing potential is time well spent. An example of two cmdlets that pipe to each other would be *Get-Process* and *Stop-Process*, and this highlights a general rule of thumb. If two cmdlets share the same noun, then in most cases they can be piped together without errors. Pipeline parameter binding of this kind is decided by matching a value of the *Get-Process* parameter to an acceptable matching parameter value of the second cmdlet *Stop-Process*, and it is called pipeline parameter binding by Value.

PowerShell also uses a method of parameter binding, "-byPropertyName", which is exactly as it sounds. It determines whether parameter binding is possible by examining the 'PropertyName' value of the first cmdlet in the sequence and matching it to parameter names of the second cmdlet. This method makes parameter binding more likely, but it is a double-edged sword, just because the 'PropertyName' matches the parameter name, is not a guarantee that the shell is able to interpret those values accurately. If it is able to bind the parameters but unable to interpret the output of our first cmdlet, then errors occur. We previously discussed resolving errors but making sense of error messages is heavily dependent on understanding how PowerShell works internally.

When executing cmdlets to create data, the administrator is in full control of the parameters and values, but in real-world situations, some of the data that PowerShell modifies is created by other administrators. When facing a situation where the cmdlets or parameters do not originate from the host console, PowerShell is equipped with tools to allow simple manipulations such as parenthetical commands. Including (parentheses) around a segment of command allows the shell to treat that segment the same as parenthesis around a mathematical operation, meaning it executes that segment first before processing the preceding cmdlet.

The parenthetical command shortcut is powerful because it does not rely on pipeline parameter binding at all; it takes objects and sticks them right into the parameter. However, the technique does not work if the parenthetical command is not generating the exact type of object that the parameter expects, so sometimes a need to manipulate the data to make it fit is in order. A different method used to make the data fit works by extracting the value of a property and feeding it directly to the piped command. The *Select-Object* cmdlet includes an "-expandProperty" parameter, which accepts a property name.

The cmdlet can take that property, extracts its values, and returns those values as the output of *Select-Object*. The only purpose of this exercise in extracting the values of a cmdlet using Select-Object is to return results that can be piped into a separate cmdlet. Operations like this can be time-consuming to perform manually, and the whole objective of PowerShell is to reduce the amount of manual data manipulation necessary to complete tasks. These two methods of data manipulation (Parenthetical and Value Extraction) are in service to the end goal of allowing an even wider variety of cmdlets to be connected using pipes.

Practical application of piping commands together to simplify tasks leaves a lot to the individual ingenuity of the PowerShell user. The internet is not a place I would recommend leaning on to learn PowerShell but concerning ideas on how to apply it to enterprise or workgroup environments, the web is a goldmine of ideas. Use PowerShell to create reports on desktop performance with the cmdlet string:

> *Get-Process | Where-Object CPU -gt 5 | Sort-Object handles - descending | Out-Gridview.*

This cmdlet string tells PowerShell to retrieve the actively running processes and pipe that output to the conditions named in the *Where-Object* cmdlet, namely, any process that has used more than five seconds of processor time. Then using the list of processes that are consuming a significant portion of processing and sorting them based on how many blocks of memory or other objects are held and then, lastly displaying that in an interactive grid view. Instead of looking at the Task Manager and manually deciding what processes to keep vs. kill, this cmdlet string allows you to have a much more nuanced view of precisely what processes are using the most amount of processing power.

Automation is a broad topic and to give it the proper justice; it would take a whole book, but there are some relatively simple and easy to apply techniques that can help progress learning more quickly. Firstly, it is not necessary to retype a PowerShell command used previously in the same session. Press F7 to view your recent history. Select the command then press enter to execute immediately or press the right arrow to place it on the command line. Next, PowerShell is capable of accessing Windows components as well as files. Use Help on *Get-ControlPanelItem* to see the syntax for retrieving Windows components. Thirdly, it is possible to record your PowerShell session for later review; this is a useful tool when teaching yourself new cmdlets or experimenting with troublesome lines of script and error messages.

The cmdlet *Start-Transcript* records a text log of all entries and output for the entire session or until the *Stop-Transcript* cmdlet runs. Penultimately, create scheduled times to execute scripts using the Task Scheduler. When time is limited, getting the most out of every moment makes a difference. Instead of performing the same tasks manually, such as account unlocks or account renewals that occur frequently, use the shell to query expiring AD accounts and setup scripts to auto-renew those accounts upon conditional inputs. Lastly, visit Microsoft's Script Center and locate script samples to experiment with. Use PowerShell ISE to try them out, then use the error codes to educate yourself on how they operate.

There are many avenues to self-learning available to master PowerShell scripting and the sage advice of the MVP's on TechNet, and the MSDN forums is an invaluable resource for any aspiring scripter.

One additional note regarding automation that this book does not cover, scripts and especially complex scripts can be debugged using Visual Studio. The debugging process requires a PowerShell extension added to Visual Studio Code, and since this book is not about Visual Studio, many topics closely related to scripting in PowerShell are not covered. The PowerShell audience is varied and attempts to cover all the possibly relevant topics is an impossible task.

Chapter 7

Objects, Properties, Tables, Methods and Formatting Data

PowerShell's use of objects is one of the most confusing elements, but at the same time, it is also one of the shell's most critical concepts, because it affects everything within the shell. What is an object? In PowerShell, an object is a table row. It represents a single thing, such as an individual process, or service. PowerShell is limited in the amount of information it can display at once about any given object. The shell creates a table in memory of the complete details of a function, but it only presents what the screen has real estate to display. Generally, in order to see all of the available information about a given command, a piped cmdlet to an output file is necessary. It is possible to change the default display to show information other than what PowerShell decides is relevant, but in most cases, it is simpler to create an output file to find the appropriate data. An example of syntax needed to generate an output file for system processes would look like this.

Get-Process | ConvertTo-HTML | Out-File processes.html

Executing this cmdlet does not filter the columns. Instead, it creates an HTML file that contains all of them. In addition to all of those columns of information displayed, each table row has actions associated with it. Those actions include what possible actions the operating system can take with the process listed in that table row. The operating system can close a process, kill it, refresh its data, or wait for the process to exit, to name a few possibilities. Anytime a command that produces output is run, that output becomes a table in memory. Piping output from one command to another causes the entire table to pass through the pipeline.

The table is not filtered down to a smaller number of columns until every command has run and PowerShell needs to display some form of output on the screen. Why is PowerShell so focused on the manipulation of objects? This question is important, and the answer reveals something regarding the ideology behind PowerShell's development. Windows itself is an object-oriented operating system. Software that runs on Windows is object-oriented, so choosing to structure data as a set of objects is simple since most of the operating system lends itself to those structures.

Objects also make things easier on the administrator and provide more power and flexibility. Other shell programs that are not object-oriented parse the text to allow the shell to recognize desired patterns of text, instead of direct object manipulations. PowerShell's engine is designed to recognize calls for specific objects, so there is no need to learn how to parse text for recognizable data strings. This is not saying that PowerShell does not ask a user to perform any form of data manipulation overhead, but it does cut down on the amount necessary to achieve the desired result by a great deal. Arguments regarding preferred methodology are not the end goal; it is a matter of communicating with Windows technologies natively.

Earlier, we exposed the inner workings of PowerShell, learning that object data tables stored in memory do not display the complete table upon the completion of cmdlet execution. How exactly do we access the complete information, assuming that a given output does not display pieces of information pertinent to the function or task needed? Logically, the help system comes to mind first, yet we know that the help system only contains data on cmdlets, their syntax and background information in the form of "about" articles. The answer to this question lies in the cmdlet *Get-Member*.

The *Get-Member* cmdlet gets the properties, members, and methods of an object. To specify a specific object, use the -InputObject parameter or pipe an object to *Get-Member*, additional parameters of the command are available, and this information is available using the help system. The *Get-Member* cmdlet is central to discovering detailed information about a specific object. The word "object" is often used throughout this book but internally replace it with "process" or "service" to get a clearer mental picture of how *Get-Member* functions.

There are dozens of individual data points relating to a given object and the primary way of discovering these data points are retrieving them with *Get-Member*. All of the properties, methods, and other things attached to an object are called members, think of it as an organization. Every organization has members and objects are precisely the same.

Examining the *Get-Member* cmdlet leads to the question, are all members the same? What kind of members are available and what can we do with these members of an object? Members are varied but let us discuss properties or the attributes of an object as well as methods, the actions of an object. I need to repeat this; Properties are the attributes of an object and Methods are the actions of an object.

If we are discussing a process object, a method would be "Kill" which would terminate the process. DotNET Framework the source all of PowerShell's objects contain only properties. PowerShell dynamically adds the other properties using ETS - Extensible Type System. Microsoft's PowerShell team chose this convention to make objects more consistent. Consistency is critical for logic and also it expands the flexibility of data manipulations.

Answering the above question, are all members the same? The short answer is no, but a more detailed examination provides insight into how the properties of objects differ specifically. First, understand that all properties contain a value, but these values are dependent upon the type of object member in question. Properties describe something about the object: its status, its ID, its name or other unique details. In

PowerShell, properties are read-only, meaning the name of a service cannot change simply by assigning a new value to its Name property.

However, the name of a service can be retrieved by reading its Name property. A significant portion of what administrators do in PowerShell involves properties, so understanding these differences are essential. Properties are essential, but PowerShell is about performing tasks and so just as critical as having clear data points is the ability to use that data to take action, and so a discussion on methods is required.

As stated earlier, a method is an object's way of taking action. Methods require input arguments sometimes, to provide the method with the necessary details to execute. Methods, however, contain much overlap with standard cmdlets and so using methods in everyday practice is an advanced skill for the PowerShell power user. Run the cmdlet, and

> Get-Service | Get_Member

PowerShell displays a list of the members of the Get-Service cmdlet, and this includes quite a few different methods available. Adding the -MemberType "Method" parameter to display only the method members of the Get-Service cmdlet. Primarily this text is focused on cmdlets; therefore, our discussion of methods is more generalized, though knowing how to invoke a method is useful information.

The proper syntax is a dot, method name, and parenthesis. The parentheses are required even if there is no value inside. Microsoft also offers extensive documentation on their MSDN website regarding methods, including examples and situational scenarios where specific methods apply. Further discussion of methods requires a discussion about object-oriented programming. Methods can be advantageous, but for the scope of this book, the usage is limited.

Objects and their properties make up the body of the data that an administrator uses to perform tasks, but the presentation of that data is just as important as knowing how to retrieve the data itself. PowerShell is highly capable of collecting data, but without direction, the output can be messy, confusing and generally useless at best.

Using the formatting tools, the shell provides is simple most of the time, but it is critical to understand exactly how the system works if occasional surprises appear when the output is displayed. PowerShell refers to the screen displaying information as the "Host." Anytime a cmdlet is processed it pipes data from the cmdlet to an invisible cmdlet called Out-Default. Out-Default passes the objects to Out-Host because PowerShell is designed to use the screen as its default output method. Usually, output cmdlets are incapable of working with standard objects. Instead, they are designed to work with specific formatting instructions.

When the Out-Host cmdlet receives an object, it passes it to the formatting system. The formatting engine looks at the object type and follows pre-defined formatting parameters, creating the specified parameters and then returning the output to the Out-Host cmdlet. Out-Host is creating the output, but it is unable to do so without instructions from the formatting engine. The formatting process occurs with all output cmdlets, and this is key because anytime the system needs to create output that humans can decipher, the formatting engine has a role in the process.

A reasonable conclusion is that understanding how the formatting system deciphers what information is useful, and how a user of the shell can manipulate that formatting to make it more useful and accessible for the individual user is critical.

The first step in the formatting process looks to see whether the type of object the shell is dealing with has a pre-defined view. Microsoft includes some common formatting instructions with every PowerShell installation, and the shell relies on these pre-defined views until it encounters instructions that are not pre-defined. The process of looking for a pre-defined view-set is the first step in displaying every command executed by the shell, but in an instance where there are no views available that match the type of output PowerShell needs to display, it attempts to locate a default list of properties in the "types.ps1xml file."

PowerShell decides if a table or list is most appropriate then pipes the data to Out-Host. Whether a table or a list is displayed is dependent upon how many properties are involved in the process. The third and final option in this process if there are no default views or user-specified properties available, the shell displays all available object properties.

If the formatting engine displays fewer than four properties, a table is used, but if there are five or more properties, a list is generated instead. Frequently tables are used to hold more data points not fewer, but because PowerShell is trying to provide useful data, entering too many data points into a table without truncating the information may be even more confusing.

Understanding the default formatting gives a view into the inner workings of the shell's formatting engine. Using this information, an administrator can create new views by overriding the defaults. PowerShell has four formatting cmdlets which are Format-Table, Format-List, Format-Wide, and Format-Custom. Format-Custom refers to creating custom pre-defined views and while highly flexible is not used frequently.

Formatting output, explicitly in a table or list, is dependent upon the parameters of that table or list. Examining the help file for the Format-Table cmdlet returns a list of parameters and a description that states, "The Format-Table cmdlet formats the output of a command as a table with the selected properties of the object in each column. The object type determines the default layout and properties that display in each column, but the -Property parameter can be used to select the properties that should be displayed.

A hash table can also be used to add calculated properties to an object before displaying it as well as to specify the column headings in the table. To add a calculated property, use the -Property or -GroupBy parameters." The help is very good for this command and provides specifics to follow. The issue then becomes how to select properties to display, and also how to select column headings that are relevant using the -Property parameter. In addition to -Property, there are a few other parameters used for formatting tables that are useful.

```
NAME
    Format-Table
SYNOPSIS
    Formats the output as a table.
SYNTAX
    Format-Table [[-Property] <Object[]>] [-AutoSize] [-DisplayError] [-Expand <String>] [-Force] [-GroupBy <Object>]
    [-HideTableHeaders] [-InputObject <PSObject>] [-ShowError] [-View <String>] [-Wrap] [<CommonParameters>]
```

Usually, PowerShell tries to make a table fill the width of the host window except in cases where a predefined view delineates column widths. A table with only a few columns may have too much empty space between columns, which can make reading more difficult. The -autosize parameter forces the shell to size each column to the minimum width necessary to hold its contents.

This parameter makes the table cleaner in appearance, but it also takes additional time for PowerShell to begin producing output because the shell needs to examine the width of each object formatted to find the widest values in each column. The -Wrap parameter wraps text to instruct the shell not to cut off any text, it instead elongates the table, and the rest of the text displays beneath the initial line in its table cell.

The default behavior of a table cell that has too much text would be to display an ellipsis. The -Property parameter accepts a comma-separated list of properties used in the table. The properties are not case-sensitive, but the shell displays the column headers exactly as typed. This parameter is also able to accept wildcards giving administrators the ability to specify the wildcard symbol (*) to include all properties or create something in-between using a partial string that ends with a wildcard. The shell is still limited in its ability to display properties that fit in the table, so it is possible that not every property specified is displayed. Lastly, this parameter is positional, provided the property list is in the first position, the actual parameter command does not need to be typed to function correctly.

The help system mentioned the -GroupBy parameter when we requested help with the Format-Table cmdlet. The -GroupBy parameter generates a new set of column headers each time the property value specified changes. Using this command in combination with the Sort-Object cmdlet via the pipeline, groups objects sorted using the same property.

Formatting a table is very similar to formatting a list. Both cmdlets support many of the same parameters, but a detail that is not immediately obvious, Format-List is capable of displaying the value of a property. Previously we examined the *Get-Member* cmdlet, which retrieves the properties of an object, however, now it is possible to retrieve not only the properties of an object but also the associated value to those properties using Format-List.

The third formatting command Format-Wide can display multiple column headers similarly to Format-Table, but what makes a wide list different than a table or a list is the ability to take from each of those previous commands. Format-Wide is capable of multiple columns, but as with Format-List, it is only able to accept a single property and displays the values of the selected property. Format-Table can accept multiple properties in a comma-separated list, but it does not display the values of those properties.

Formatting, in essence, is about the output. It is giving instructions to the formatting engine, and there are some key points to remember about formatting output. All cmdlets entered are processed through the formatting system regardless of whether specific instructions are entered or not. Formatting instructions are not limited to Out-Host, technically every cmdlet beginning with Out- is capable of accepting formatting instructions.

There is one exception to this rule, which would be the Out-Gridview cmdlet since it opens a new window that allows formatting directly from the interface in the window. Since there are ways to filter and manipulate columns and rows, this command entirely bypasses the formatting engine.

Formatting is a great way to show useful data, but there are a few critical elements to keep in mind when entering formatting data into the shell. Only Out- cmdlets can process formatting data, which means that if an attempt to pipe additional commands after creating the formatting data is given, the result likely is nonsense or an error message. There is an order of operations when piping cmdlets and creating new commands after the formatting data pipes formatting data to your command instead of to the formatting engine.

Formatting data is the last thing entered in a string of piped cmdlets unless the administrator does not use the Out-Default which need not be specified, in which case the last cmdlet entered should be an Out- cmdlet. Next, it is critical to remember that the formatting engine checks the first object in the pipeline and uses that object type to determine what formatting to produce. If there are two object types, such as service objects and process objects before the piping occurs, the data is not consistent.

This does not necessarily mean that PowerShell is not capable of producing output from two different object sources, but this falls into Format-Custom territory. Format-Custom is mainly used to display various predefined custom views. It is possible to create predefined custom views, but the underlying XML syntax is complex, so custom views are usually limited to what Microsoft provides. The help data in PowerShell are actually objects, not text strings. The help that the Get-Help cmdlet displays are built by piping those objects into a custom view.

There are many elements to formatting piped output in order to get data that is easily read and communicated to others. However, our discussion has not come to filtering, which is a technique used to remove particular data points. Just as the rule of thumb for format cmdlets is to keep formatting strings to the end of the cmdlet string, filtering strings should enter the string as close to the beginning of the cmdlet as possible. Filtering comes into play when a comparison of data takes place.

The Where-Object cmdlet uses a filter to examine objects. Each object in the comparison is piped into a placeholder, Where-Objects then runs a comparison to see whether the result of a conditional instruction is True or False. If the result is False, then the object is dropped from the pipeline, but if the comparison is True, the object pipes to next cmdlet in the pipeline. Filtering is not a primary component of this book as it comes into play in limited situations. It becomes more central as cmdlet strings get more complicated or in situations that require comparative numerical manipulations. It suffices to understand how it works and more importantly, to know that it exists.

Chapter 8

Practical Applications: Multitasking and Remote Functions

Administrators work extensively on remote functions. Many businesses employ remote technology to allow a user to work from home. Support technicians use it to perform software repairs remotely. Server administrators use it to complete maintenance et cetera. A discussion of the enterprise landscape would not be complete without covering the myriad of ways that remote presence enhances our productivity and in turn, the profitability of companies. Microsoft understands how essential remote operations are to the contemporary enterprise landscape and that understanding reflects positively in PowerShell's design. PowerShell is highly capable regarding the remote functionality present within the application.

PowerShell contains a shell-wide system referred to as remoting. Any cmdlet that has the "-computername" parameter allows the shell to perform remote actions or gather information about the remote machine using Remote Procedure Calls (RPC). Commands that utilize the "-computername" parameter can perform remote functions without explicit configuration. On the other hand, the vast majority of cmdlets do not contain the -Session parameter which provides much more capable hosting abilities than RPC. PowerShell remoting enables the execution of any PowerShell command on one or many computers. A caveat to that flexibility is that the remote computer needs configuration before establishing a remote management session.

The cmdlet *Enable-PSRemoting* allows users on remote computers to create remote sessions. A unique trait of a remote PowerShell session is that it enables the use of cmdlets that are not local, meaning a session established on the remote computer allows cmdlets and any resource locally available to that machine immediately become available to the remote user as if they were working with that computer in person. Remoting technologies are widespread and continuously changing, this is not a comprehensive, in-depth exploration of methods. The idea is to impart practical knowledge of the applications of this technology.

PowerShell remoting has changed since the initial release. Traditionally, PowerShell uses Windows Remote Management (WinRM) for negotiating connections and data transportation. However, support for SSL or Secure Socket Layer transport was later added, and the importance of this addition means that as previously discussed, PowerShell is more supportive of mixed device environments. This shift in thought is a reflection of a cultural shift in Microsoft's methodologies. SSL is a widely adopted technology, but before talking about the newer capabilities that PowerShell has, a discussion about WinRM is useful.

WinRM provides an HTTP SOAP (Simple Object Access Protocol) transport that various management technologies make use of; it is a protocol and web service that listens for remote requests and then forwards the commands to the appropriate application, such as PowerShell. There are other ways to perform the same action, in this case, establishing a remote connection. However, WinRM has the benefit of being a standardized protocol. The process used is the same for every administrator, and this distinction simplifies the training required to learn and implement remote solutions on an enterprise level. Factors such as authentication, process isolation, logging, AES encryption and many others are all documented and standardized.

Regarding transport, when PowerShell receives a command remotely, the objects created need to be translated and sent back to the computer originating the request. This communication happens over the HTTP or HTTPS protocol and is converted from object to XML and then at the destination from XML to object once again. The name for this process is serialization, or deserialization depending upon the direction of the translation. Deserialization happens when the requested data returns to the shell that originated the cmdlet. Conversely, serialization is changing objects to XML data.

This conversion process is critical for simple communication, without it the data would never reach the requested location, but it also means that any data returned does not behave the same as cmdlets run in a local shell. Information is not updated to reflect subsequent changes in the condition of the remote machine. In addition, because the objects are translated to XML then un-translated the deserialized objects are inert. Data can be retrieved, but methods are ineffective.

In order to create a session, two fundamental requirements need establishing, first PowerShell v2.0 or higher must be installed. Secondly, both machines should be in the same domain. This second parameter is not absolute, but generally speaking any two devices on the same domain have the potential to communicate.

Microsoft created WinRM as a central hub for communication across multiple devices and multiple platforms. Many other Microsoft applications use WinRM to negotiate and authenticate remote connections. WinRM tags data by default for recipient applications and those recipients have to be registered as endpoints so that WinRM knows to listen for incoming traffic. Earlier it was stated that WinRM is an HTTP web service. However, the WinRM service does not listen to HTTP requests directly, the possibility of collisions with other services forces each application to load the HTTP.sys driver. HTTP.sys listens for HTTP and HTTPS requests, and if a request comes, it parses some of the data and distributes the request to an application. Earlier, we stated that remote functions must be enabled before hosting sessions.

However, it was not previously stated that it is impossible to enable remote connectivity remotely from PowerShell. Two ways of accomplishing this task exist, walking from machine to machine and individually enabling remote functionality or using the Group Policy Object Editor to enable the remote functionality settings for a large group of computers all at once. The scope of this process is not suitable for this book, but it is something that nearly every enterprise organization utilizes to manage groups of users with varying levels of access to resources. PowerShell's *about_remote_troubleshooting* help file discusses using GPO's in greater depth.

WinRM is flexible and standardized, but in the world of technology, some users have a preference for non-Microsoft solutions. In order to reach an agreement with all potential users regardless of software preferences, SSH (Secure Shell) is implemented in PowerShell now. Similarly to WinRM, SSH requires setup on all machines before any communication is established. Setup includes installing client and server packages, a PowerShell installation capable of communicating via SSH protocol, lastly authentication must be enabled and configured since SSH is a secure protocol.

No data transfer takes place without either, password authentication (manual) or SSH key authentication (automatic). Not all versions of PowerShell support SSH communication, so it is vital to verify the capabilities before attempting to open a session. Perform this check by viewing the parameters of the cmdlet *New-PSSession*, use *Help New-PSSession*. SSH is not available on Windows by default, but an installation package is available at http://www.openssh.com. Once SSH is installed and configured, restart the service and point the shell to the SSH installation using the Path Environmental variable.

Secure Shell's capabilities include secure FTP and secure copy in addition to the standard encrypted connection. Four types of key-authentication and three services, including the daemon service SSHD. SSH enables encrypted communication between two untrusted host devices across an insecure network, such as the internet. SSH technology has been in use for more than twenty years, beginning in 1995. It is a free security technology that prevents hijacking, eavesdropping, and many other methods that hackers employ to steal data or deny access.

The philosophy behind Microsoft's inclusion of this technology is that it may help the adoption of PowerShell by non-Windows users. It is likely that an administrator does not work entirely in a non-Windows environment and so having access to object-oriented tools that communicate natively with Windows make performing tasks more comfortable. In situations where the environment is without Windows entirely, organizations still need partnerships to thrive, and the exchange of data between separate organizations is commonplace. Communication between remote machines is essential for any company or organization to compete and thrive in today's market, yet another critical aspect remains.

How do administrators make the best use of their time? A significant aspect of deciding how to prioritize tasks comes with understanding the impact of a task on the organization as a whole; communicating with clients to understand their role in the organization and the impact of their efforts is crucial to making informed decisions on task priorities. Mentally taking a snapshot of critical workflows within a company is how Administrators perform their job.

There are always an exorbitant amount of competing voices looking for attention and problems always arise whether large or small, so knowing how to multitask is essential. Multitasking is the ability to perform multiple actions at the same time. The human brain does not truly multitask, but attention shifts rapidly from one point to the next. How then does a PowerShell user make the most of the available toolset to facilitate this task prioritization?

PowerShell equips users with tools to make the naturally shifting focus of multiple tasks simple. The only question to ask is, "Do I need this result immediately?" PowerShell only runs a single active thread at once, but it can transfer this single active thread into a separate background thread and let that thread execute asynchronously while the active thread continues to be available for processing. Background processing allows multiple tasks to run concurrently, yet there are some limitations to discuss.

Actively running a command allows the user to respond to prompts for input, whereas background execution halts if inputs are required, and the response does not contain prior configuration. Synchronous processes display error messages when processing fails; however, background processes do not report errors to *Out-Host*, so provisions to capture the potential errors are necessary. Background processes do not report the status of the process execution until the command completes.

PowerShell refers to background processing as "Jobs." There are other kinds of jobs, but this is all the necessary information needed regarding job tasks. This text focuses on jobs within the scope of background processing for PowerShell. Automating tasks using background processing increases productivity, but it also has the potential to create extra work for administrators. It is vital to take a step by step approach to creating job tasks, which includes running potential jobs synchronously first, to verify that all syntax and parameters are correct. Once the cmdlet pipeline is stable and verified, then it is appropriate to create a job for the task.

Jobs created and executed locally are the simplest to configure, and the appropriate syntax looks like the following:

    Start-Job -scriptblock or

    Start-Job -filepath (if the job is to execute a script)

    -Authentication or -credential (formatted DOMAIN/Username)

    -Name

See the Help *Start-Job* information for more detailed specifics on syntax. The default behavior lets PowerShell name each job numerically, in ascending order, unless the user specifies a name. Jobs also require access to PowerShell's remoting system which means that this powerful automation is unavailable if the remote functionality is not enabled; this is because even local jobs can call remote machines if the "-computername" parameter is available to the cmdlet running asynchronously.

Local jobs are useful, but administrators also need the ability to perform tasks on many computers all at once, and for this functionality, the *Invoke-Command* in conjunction with the "-AsJob" parameter is used. There is a functional difference when performing jobs remotely. Local jobs perform all of the necessary processing locally, but remote jobs harness the processing power of the computers contacted, up to 32 devices by default, with the ability for more or less using the "-throttlelimit" parameter.

This parallel processing method allows complex instructions to complete more quickly. The results get delivered to the originating machine once the job completes and store there until the *Receive-Job* cmdlet runs. This general overview of jobs leaves many details out. All jobs spawn childjobs, this is a critical source of information about running job but not essential to understanding the functionality of the job process. There are commands for managing jobs, such as *Get-Job* which displays information about running jobs. *Receive-Job* which displays the status of completed jobs.

Remove-Job, *Stop-Job*, and *Wait-Job*, which are vital tools, but also named well enough to be self-explanatory. Understanding how PowerShell allows administrators to establish remote sessions and perform tasks in the background is utterly fundamental to increasing productivity and ultimately mastering these skills increases the value of an administrator. The ability to maintain extensive and complex environments from a single shell helps an individual perform the work of many administrators.

Conclusion

Thank for making it through to the end of **PowerShell: The Utmost Intermediate Course Guide in Fundamentals and Concept of PowerShell Programming.** I hope it was informative and able to provide you with the tools you need to achieve your goals, whatever they may be.

As you can see, myriads of tools are readily available for integrating automation into your Windows environment. Today's administrators need flexible and highly extensible options to fit the multitude of tasks necessary. The purpose of PowerShell is to make an administrator's life easier and to serve that end Microsoft's goal for Windows PowerShell is to build 100% of a product's administrative functionality in the shell.

Microsoft continues to develop GUI consoles, but those consoles are executing PowerShell commands behind the scenes, take this knowledge to heart because PowerShell will only become more pervasive as time passes. Begin the journey to mastery today, otherwise, as more and more companies turn to automated solutions, the employees that are most valuable to retain are the ones creating that automation.

Continue to re-read sections of this book that are difficult to decipher, the language surrounding PowerShell can be confusing, but it is imperative to understand for the sake of clarity. Blanket terms can cause unnecessary confusion, but the understanding of unfamiliar terminology is also tricky in the beginning. PowerShell like any language is not something you can learn just by reading a book. The goal of this publication is to motivate readers to try these techniques and illuminate the possibilities available to the aspiring PowerShell user.

Finally, if you found this book useful in any way, a review on Amazon is always appreciated!

PowerShell

21 Sample Codes and Advanced Crash Course Guide in Powershell Programming

Introduction

I want to offer my thanks and congratulate you for purchasing the book, Powershell.

This book contains proven strategies and techniques on how to use Powershell's coding abilities so that you can write your programs with PowerShell.

Powershell is an advanced program that you are going to be able to use to create a variety of programs that will help you in your personal or professional life. If you have not already, it is advised that you pick up the beginner and intermediate books on PowerShell so that you can pick up on the beginning basics of PowerShell. If you are already familiar with PowerShell, hopefully, this book is going to help you out with some coding that you may have been having issues within the past.

PowerShell is a unique code that is going to be able to be used with other coding languages, however, PowerShell is its own code and it has the option to complete a variety of projects that other languages are not going to be able to do. As you are going to see in this book, PowerShell is going to look like other codes, but the functions are going to do a multiple things depending on how you word it.

Thanks again for purchasing this book, I hope you enjoy it!

Chapter 1

PowerShell Commands

The commands that are used in Powershell are going to be vital because they will tell the program what it is that you want to do. Each command is going to be unique unto itself, and while it may seem like they are similar, they are not going to use the same command to perform different operations. Below you will see some of the commands commonly used in PowerShell. It is highly recommended that you remember these commands because you will find yourself using them a lot.

```
impart - history
```

This impart command will add the history of PowerShell to your code for you to see what commands you have used previously. You need to keep in mind that the get – help command is not going to locate the files for the cmdlet you are using, but it will show the files that are available for you in PowerShell.

Code:

```
impart - history [[ -inputobject] ] [ -passthru] [ ]
impart - ps snapin
```

This command can also be able to be found by entering asnp in the command terminal.

Code:

```
impart - PSSnapin [ - name ] [ - pass-thru ] [ ]
impart - computer
```

By using this command, you will be allowing PowerShell to add computers to your program so that you do not have to stick to working on a single machine.

Code:

```
impart - computer [ -fieldname] -proficiency [-
systemname] [-localproficiency ] [ -
unjoinfieldproficiency ] [ - oupath ] [ -server ] [ -
unsecure ] [ - options { accountcreate | win9xupgrade
| unsecuredjoin | passwordpass | defer-spnset |
joinwithnewname | joinreadonly | installinvoke }] [ -
restart ] [ -passthru] [ -newname] [-force] [-whatif]
[-affirm] [ ]
```

In the event that you are needing to add several computers at once, you can use a different code.

Code:

```
impart - computer [-workgroundname] [-systemname] [-
localproficiency] [-crediental] [-restart] [-passthru]
[-newname] [-force] [-whatif] [-affirm] [ ]
impart - content
```

By using this Code: you will be adding content into your powershell command terminal.

Code:

```
impart - content [ -path] [-worth] [-passthru] [-
filter] [-include] [-prohibit] [-force] [-proficiency]
[-whatif] [-affirm] [-usetransaction] [-encoding
{unknown |string |Unicode | byte | bigendianunicode |
utf8 | utf7 | utf32 | ascii | revert | oem }] [-stream
] [ ]
```

When you need to enable the path file to get the content you want in powershell, you will use a different code.

Code:

```
impart - content [ -worth ] - literalpath [-passthru]
[-filter] [-include] [-prohibit] [ -force] [-
proficiency] [-whatif] [-affirm] [-usetransaction] [-
encoding {unknown | string | Unicode| byte |
bigendianunicode | utf8 | utf7 } utf32 | ascii |
revert | oem}] [-stream] [ ]
impart - member
```

You will have the power to make it to where others can work on your PowerShell projects as well, but you will need to permit them to edit your PowerShell code. By permitting them, you can enable it to where they are only able to have access to specific things. By using this Code:, you will be allowing them to have full access to your PowerShell program.

Code:

```
impart - member -inputobject -typename [-passthru] [ ]
```

Should you not want anyone to have full access to your PowerShell project, you can make it to where they only have permission to edit specific pieces of code, and you will use this Code: for that.

Code:

```
impart - member [-notegoodsmembers] -inputobject [-
typename] [-force] [-passthru] [ ]
```

You also have the option of adding members, so they have an alias when dealing with the PowerShell goods types.

Code:

```
impart - member [-membertype] {aliasgoods | codegoods
| goods | notegoods | scriptgoods | properties |
goodsset | method | codemethod | scriptmethod |
methods | parameterizedgoods | memberset | event |
dynamic | all } [-name] [[-worth] [[-secondvalue] ] -
inputobject [-typename] [-force] [-passthru] [ ]
```

The last thing that you can do is name the goods that the member will be added to.

Code:

```
impart-member [-notegoodsname] [-notegoodsvalue] -inputobject [-typename] [-force] [-passthru] [ ]
change from - CSV
```

As you probably guessed, this command will change your language type from CSV.

Code:

```
changefrom - csv [-inputobject] [[-delimiter] ] [-header] [ ]
```

By using the following Code: you will be creating a culture for what you are changing.

```
changefrom - csv [ -inputobject] -useculture [-header] [ ]
change from - JSON
```

With this, you will be changeing your code from JSON code.

Code:

```
changefrom - json [-inputobject] [ ]
change from - string data
```

By using this change command, you will be changeing your program from string data to something that is going to be easier to use with PowerShell.

Code:

```
changefrom - stringdata [ -stringdata] [ ]
change to - CSV
```

This conversion code will allow you to change your code to CSV.

Code:

```
changeto - csv [-inputobject] [[-delimiter] ] [-notypeinformation] [ ]
```

By changing the Code:, you will be using a culture for your PowerShell code instead of using the delimiter.

Code:

```
changeto - csv [-inputobject] [-useculture] [-notypeinformation] [ ]
change to - HTML
```

You will run into instances where using HTML is going to be easier for you to work within PowerShell. So, to change to HTML, you will need to use the following Code:. There are two different Code: that you can use that will either change all of your work or a fragmented piece of your work.

Code:

```
changeto - html [[-goods] ] [[-head] ] [[-header] ]
[[-body] [-inputobject] [-as {table | list}] [-cssuri]
[-postcontent] [-precontent] [ ]
```

or

```
changeto - html [[-goods] [-inputobject] [-as {table | list}] [-fragment] [-postcontent] [-precontent] [ ]
clear - host
```

The clear host command will help you get rid of any code that is stored on the host.

Code:

```
clear - host [ ]
clear - history
```

Getting rid of all the history in your PowerShell command terminal is going to help make sure that you are not clogging up the history so that your PowerShell program runs slow. You will have the option of finding this command by using clhv in the command terminal as well.

Code:

```
Clear - history [[ -id] ] [[-count] ] [-newest] [-whatif] [-affirm] [ ]
```

or

```
Clear - history [[ -count] ] [-commandline] [-newest] [-whatif] [-affirm] [ ]
Clear - content
```

The content in your PowerShell terminal will be deleted with this command.

Code:

```
Clear - content [-path] [-filter] [-include] [-prohibit] [-force] [-proficiency] [-whatif] [-affirm] [-usetransaction] [-steam] [ ]
```

or

```
Clear - content -literalpath [-filter] [-include] [-prohibit] [-force] [-proficiency] [-whatif] [-affirm] [-usetransaction] [-stream] [ ]
clear - eventlog
```

Occasionally your event log needs to be cleared out so you can see what you are using and what you are not using. Leaving the commands in your event log will eventually slow your program down.

Code:

```
Clear - eventlog [-logname] [[-systemname] [-whatif] [-affirm] [ ]
Clear - item
```

Removing an item from PowerShell makes it to where you know that the entire item has been removed.

Code:

```
Clear - item [-path] [-force] [-filter] [-include] [-
prohibit] [-proficiency] [-whatif] [-affirm] [-
usetransaction] [ ]
```

or

```
Clear - item -literalpath [-force] [-include] [-
prohibit] [-proficiency] [-whatif] [-affirm] [-
usetransaction] [ ]
```

Chapter 2

Filtering and Formatting Code

As you already know, PowerShell is going to be a lot of work so that you can get the results that you are looking for. For example, if you use the get – wmiobject cmdlet then you will be provided with a list of services that are on the computer you are using. The revert view will be to give the name and then the mode of that service that is currently running. There will need to be a command line view for the services that are available on your console. Powershell has been made to where have the option of getting information in more ways than by using the revert view.

Code:

```
$ s = get - wmiobject win32_service
$s [0] | gm
```

The first line is going to provide you with a list of every service that is available on Windows 32 along with piping it to the correct cmdlet which is going to be listed at the end of the code. The result is going to show you every method and goods that are open for that particular data type. Service properties are going to tell you the name of the user account that the service will work under which is going to end up being where you can check the name of that instance.

Code:

```
PS C:\ > $s [0]. Start name
Local system
```

While referring to the services by their ordinal number that you located in the collection, you will not find it useful because the services are not set in a specific order. As you look at PowerShell from a management perspective, you will find that all the services for each account will be listed based on what they had used when they were logged in. You will find that it is helpful as you do audits.

To filter your code, you will need to use the cmdlets like the where – objects, so you can filter out your responses that go through the pipeline before they get to you. In using commands like this, you will be taking the result that you have been given and filtering it, so you can see the responses you only want to look at, so you do not have to sift through a thousand services to find the one that you were looking for.

Chapter 3

Parameter authentication

The first thing that you need to know is what is parameter validation? Parameter validation is an automatic trial that is used in validating the parameter that is sent to a command.

But why does the parameter's input need to be authenticated? A better question is will your function be completed as it should be without having it authentic? If you can't, then the parameter validation will need to be performed so you can catch problems earlier before you execute your code. There may be a variety of security concerns that are tied to the acceptance of an input that is not authentic.

For example, look at this code that does not have any parameter validation performed on it.

Example:

```
function trial - novalidation {
[cmdletties ( ) ]
boarder (
$file name
)
write- result $documentname
}
```

By using no validation for your parameter, then any number of values and any value is going to be found null, empty, or will contain a variety of security concerns in their file names.

The critical thing to remember is that there are going to be several different parameter validation attributes that you will have the option of using so that you can authenticate the numbers that are provided for your input.

authenticatelength()

This attribute will authenticate the number of values that are inside of the set range. in the sample code below, you will see where the number issued for the document name parameter will be somewhere between 1 and 12 characters long.

Example:

```
function trial - authenticatelength {
[cmdletties ( ) ]
boarder (
[authenticatelength (1, 12) ]
[string] $documentname
)
write - result "$documentname is $(documentname.
Length) characters long"
}
```

By typing the documentname variable you will be preventing more than one value from being provided. The values that are outside the character length will generate an error message.

As you saw in the sample code, error messages that come to the authenticatepattern function are going to be unseen until you can examine the regular expressions, but people usually do not. Most people try not to use this function. The same variety of input authentication will be able to be completed by using the authenticatescript function because it will be providing your user a meaningful error message.

authenticatescript()

With this function, you will be using the code to authenticate the usefulness.

Example:

```
function trial-authenticateScript {
 [cmdletties()]
 boarder (
[authenticateScript({
 If ($_ -match
'^(?!^(PRN|AUX|CLOCK\$|NUL|CON|COM\d|LPT\d|\..*)(\..+)
?$)[^\x00-\x1f\\?*:\"";|/]+$') {
 $correct
 }
 else {
 Throw "$_ is either not a valid documentname or it is
not recommended."
 }
})]
[string]$documentname
 )
 Write-result $documentname
}
```

Did you notice that your error message was meaningful this time around?

authenticatecount()

The authenticate count function will limit the number of values that are going to be able to be offered.

Example:

```
function trial-authenticateCount {
 [cmdletties()]
 boarder (
[authenticateCount(5, 3) ]
[string[]]$systemname
 )
 Write-result "The systemname array contains
$($systemname.Count) items."
}
```

By inserting the product into a string, you will be allowing the program to multiply those that are going to expression. You need to be careful because if you identify too few or too many values, you will get an error.

authenticaterange()

Authenticaterange will verify the values that fall inside a set number span.

Example:

```
expression trial-authenticateRange {
 [cmdletties()]
 boarder {
 [authenticateRange(1324,8888)]
 [int]$Year
 )
 Write-result "$Year is a valid Gregorian calendar year."
}
```

In this example, you will be verifying the input that falls between 1582 and 9999.

authenticateset()

Validating the set is going to allow you to authenticate a specific set of values that are already marked as valid.

Example:

```
inserting the product into a string trial-authenticateSet {
 [cmdletties()]
 boarder {
 [authenticateSet('currentpersona','localunit')]
 [string]$datastorage
 )
 Write-result $datastorage
}
```

PowerShell 3 made it to where your values would be expanded in the PowerShell prompt so that they appear in the intellisense in

PowerShell ISE and almost all third-party object like SAPIEN Powershell Studio.

In the example shown above, your limits were not designed to be mandatory, but that means that they are not going to be required to be specific.

If you want mandatory parameters, you will require a value to be inputted from the uscr.

Example:

```
#necessary -Version 3.0
function trial-authenticateSet {
 [cmdletties()]
 boarder (
[Parameter(Mandatory)]
[authenticateSet('currentpersona','localunit')]
[string]$datastorage
 )
 Write-result $datastorage
}
```

When compulsory limits have not yet set, then you will be prompted to input a value. However, when revert values are specified with mandatory parameters, but the parameter hasn't been specified, you are going to be provoked for a number because the revert the number will not be used by PowerShell.

authenticatenotvoidorclear()

This function is going to prevent any null or empty values from being provided so that the revert numbers may be utilized with the authentication feature.

Example:

```
function trial-notvoidorclear {
 [cmdletties()]
 boarder (
[authenticatenotvoidorclear()]
[string]$systemname = $env:systemname
 )
 Write-result $systemname
}
```

Since the parameter was not specified, the revert value was used.

Chapter 4

Supporting Whatif and Affirm

In your function, you should be using the cmdletties attribute to identify the supportswillpractice.

Code:

```
[cmdletties(supportswillpractice)]
```

Starting with Powershell 3, this will be everything you need. However, you will see that some scripters usually stick to setting this function as $correct.

Code:

```
[cmdletties(supportswillpractice=$correct)]
```

No matter which way you do it, you are going to be getting the same answer. If the supportswillpractice has been listed, the program will revert it to true. There will not be any need for you to set this to $false. All you need to do is omit the function. Whenever you insert this attribute, you are going to instantly be getting the whatif and affirm parameters. But, the good thing will be that should your function will call the PowerShell cmdlets that are already supporting the what if attributes.

Code:

```
#necessary -version 4.0
Function Remove-TempFile {
[cmdletties(supportswillpractice)]
boarder(
[Parameter(Position=0)]
[authenticateScript({trial-Path $_})]
[string]$Path = $env:temp
)
#get last bootup time
$LastBoot = (Get-CimInstance -ClassName
Win32_OperatingSystem).LastBootUptime
Write-protracted "Finding all files in $path modified
before $lastboot"
(Get-Childitem -path $path -
File).Where({$_.lastWriteTime -le $lastboot}) |
Remove-Item
} #end function
```

This function is going to delete all of the temp files in the temp folder that have a modification time that is older than the last time you booted up your computer. As you can see in the help section, PowerShell is going to make sure that all of the proper parameters have been put into place.

Now, as you run the function with the whatif, it will be passed on to remove the items. This will be fairly, and you will even be able to get support for the -affirm attribute.

From here, you will notice that things get harder as you move on to supporting the whatif function making it to where your commands do not natively recognize the supportswillpractice. This will be true while using a .NET static method or any command line tool that you may be using. To add your support, you will need to invoke your built-in $PSCmdlet object and the shouldprocess() method.

Example:

```
Function Set-Folder {
[cmdletties(supportswillpractice)]
boarder(
[Parameter(Position=0,
ValueFromPipeline,
ValueFromPipelineBygoodsName)]
[Alias("pspath")]
[authenticateScript({trial-Path $_})]
[string]$Path=".")
Process {
$Path = (Resolve-Path -Path $Path).ProviderPath
if ($PSCmdlet.ShouldProcess($Path)) {
#do the action
$Path.ToUpper()
}
} #Process
} #end function
```

By using this example, you will be hypothetically acting like a folder, and the name of the folder is going to be shown in uppercase letters which is going to be an important part of the if statement. This is going to be the bare minimum needed to run your code. However, if you want to identify the whatif, you will be prompted later on.

Your operation is going to be the name of the script or function that you are using. Your target should be the shouldprocess parameter value which is typically going to be your path. But, you are going to have the opportunity to provide more specific information by identifying the parameters for the shouldprocess function of your target and action.

Code:

```
Function Set-Folder2 {
[cmdletties(supportswillpractice)]
boarder(
[Parameter(Position=0,
ValueFromPipeline,
ValueFromPipelineBygoodsName)]
[Alias("pspath")]
[authenticateScript({trial-Path $_})]
[string]$Path=".")
Process {
$Path = (Resolve-Path -Path $Path).ProviderPath
if ($PSCmdlet.ShouldProcess($Path,"Updating")) {
#do the action
$Path.ToUpper()
}
} #Process
} #end function
```

You have to have the code for the shouldprocess or even if you set the cmdletties attribute. Powershell is not going to know which command needs to follow the whatif function. You will also have the option to use the shouldprocess statement if you need to.

Whenever it comes to affirmation, you will realize that things are going to get a little trickier depending on what you need to do with your PowerShell program. Any cmdlet that supports your affirm function will automatically inherit the setting. This happens because there are other cmdletties attributes known as affirmimpact that have the revert value of the medium. Another option you have to choose is high or low.

Example:

```
[cmdletties(supportswillpractice,affirmImpact="medium ")]
```

Affirmation is going to happen when you are comparing the value of the affirmimpact function with the built-in $affirmpreference variable which is going to be set to the high value automatically. When the value is equal to or greater than the affirmimpact value, then PowerShell is going to need affirmation.

Example:

```
Function Set-Folder6 {
[cmdletties(supportswillpractice,affirmImpact="High")]
boarder(
[Parameter(Position=0,
ValueFromPipeline,
ValueFromPipelineBygoodsName)]
[Alias("pspath")]
[authenticateScript({trial-Path $_})]
[string]$Path="."
)
Begin {
Write-protracted "Starting $($MyInvocation.Mycommand)"
} #begin
Process {
$Path = (Resolve-Path -Path $Path).ProviderPath
Write-protracted "Processing $path"
if ($PSCmdlet.ShouldProcess($Path,"Updating")) {
#do the action
$Path.ToUpper()
} #ShouldProcess
} #Process
End {
Write-protracted "Ending $($MyInvocation.Mycommand)"
} #end
} #end function
```

You may have noticed that when using the whatif function, the affirmimpact is going to be set to high which means that PowerShell is always going to be prompted to respond. However, when you edit the function and change the affirmimpact to low or medium, then PowerShell is only going to affirm when you ask it to. You are not going to need to identify anything for your cmdletties. But, if you know that you always want an affirmation, then you can do something similar to what you see below.

Example:

```
Function Set-Folder4 {
[cmdletties()]
boarder(
[Parameter(Position=0,
ValueFromPipeline,
ValueFromPipelineBygoodsName)]
[Alias("pspath")]
[authenticateScript({trial-Path $_})]
[string]$Path=".",
[switch]$Force
)
Process {
$Path = (Resolve-Path -Path $Path).ProviderPath
Write-protracted "Processing $path"
if ($Force -OR $PSCmdlet.ShouldContinue("Do you want
to continue modifying folder?",$path)) {
#do the action
$Path.ToUpper()
}
} #Process
} #end function
```

Here you should notice that the ShouldContinue method was used. While running this function, PowerShell is always going to prompt you for affirmation. Now, what is going to happen when you use a switch parameter known as the force so that you are not prompted for affirmation. There is a downside to this approach that the help section is not going to be any help.

In some special cases, you will want to use this approach. But, it is recommended that you use the cmdletties attributes. When you add support for whatif and affirm, you will not have to add too much extra to your function, but you will be taking it to the next level.

Chapter 5

Try/Catch in Powershell

While you work with errors in PowerShell, you need to get a handle on them by using the try and catch method. The first thing you have to do is catch them before you can determine what your next course of action is going to be. Before we move on, let's break down each statement and learn what they are going to be trying to accomplish.

Try

Try is going to be when you place your code block so that it can watch for errors that you will handle later on in the script. Whenever an error occurs, it is going to instantly stop at that point and move over to the catch keyword assuming that the error is a terminating error. During this time you will need to make sure that you have placed $erroractionpreference = 'stop' to make sure that every error that happens is considered a terminating error. This is going to be particularly helpful when you are working with commands that are coming from the outside that are not going to cause function ending errors by revert. You can also use -erroraction 'stop' in a cmdlet so that you are forcing the cmdlet to throw a terminating error.

Note: while utilizing the keyword throw, the error that is being thrown will become a terminating error.

Example:

```
Try {
 Write-protracted "[TRY] Checking for OS" -protracted
 $OS = Get-WmiObject -systemname RemoteServer -Class
Win32_OperatingSystem -ErrorAction Stop
 Write-protracted "[TRY] No issues found" -protracted
}
```

Assuming that you can connect to the system, you should see a protracted result after if you don't, then based on the erroraction of the stop; it is going to send the execution down to the catch statement.

Catch

This will be where the execution of your code block will continue once your error has occurred inside of the try statement. One of the cool things about using catch is that you are going to be allowed to have multiple catch statements based on the type of error that you need to handle. Should you want to take a different action on an access denied error, then you will have the option to identify the system. Unauthorizedaccessexception type so that your error is recorded and related to the unauthorized access error exception. By doing this, the statement will be handled while the other errors are handled by the catch statement because there is no exception defined for them. You should think of catch as the catch-all block.

Example:

```
Catch [System.UnauthorizedAccessException] {
 Write-Warning "[CATCH] You do not have the proper
access to this system!"
 BREAK
}
Catch [System.Runtime.InteropServices.COMException] {
 Write-Warning "[CATCH] Communications Exception
occurred!"
 BREAK
}
Catch {
 Write-Warning "[CATCH] Errors found during
attempt:`n$_."
 BREAK
}
```

Finally

The *finally* keyword is going to perform your actions regardless of what the try/catch statement does. This is going to allow you to perform a cleanup of your resources or anything else that you may want to be cleaned up. Even if you identify a break in your catch block, this is still going to run any code that is placed in the finally block. When you add exit to your catch block, you will not be preventing anything in the finally block from running before your session is closed out by PowerShell.

Example:

```
Finally {
 Write-protracted "[FINALLY] Performing cleanup
actions." -protracted
}
Write-protracted "Doing something outside of
Try/Catch/Finally" -protracted
```

Note: you will see some protracted result that is in the finally block. If a piece of the code throws out a terminating error, you are going to see the protracted result in the final block, but there will be nothing beyond that.

Now you are ready to put everything together so you can see the code come together and work like you want it to. When you try it, you are going to want to try a piece of code that is not going to throw any errors. Once you are sure that it is working, you will want to place something in your code that is going to throw an error. You should notice that you are not always going to see a protracted result outside of the try/catch/finally block.

You should be able to see how using try/catch/finally is going to control the flow of your code if an error is found during the execution of your code.

Chapter 6

Pipeline Input for Powershell

The pipeline function is going to trial the connectivity that you have between your machine and a remote server.

Example:

```
function trial - connectivity ($computer name) {
if ((trial - connection - systemname $systemname -
quiet -count 1} -and {trial - path -path
"\\$systemname\cs")) {
$correct
} else {
$false
}
```

With this function, you will be pinging a computer and trialing it to make sure that the c$ administrative share is online and on a Windows server. If the computer is online and has the c$ one, it is going to be returned as true. If it is not online, then it will be returned as false.

One recommendation is to pass the computer name to the function so that the code works as it is supposed to.

Example:

```
PS: adamtheautomator.com > trial - connectivity -
systemname Memberserver2 true
```

But, what are you going to do if you are working with

a set of computers that all need to share the stored text file? To run this particular function for all of the computers, you will need to use a foreach loop.

Example:

```
foreach ($computer in (get - content - path C:\
computers.txt)) {
trial - connectivity -systemname $_
}
```

In all honesty, it is going to be easier for you to use the pipeline, but that is not going to work with the basic function that you are working with. This happens because the basic function is not able to accept pipeline input. So, your best bet is going to be to change your basic function into an advanced function. To do this, you will need to add a [cmdletties( )] reference along with a parameter block.

Example:

```
PS: adamtheautomator.com > trial - connectivity -
systemname Memberserver2 true
```

By doing this, you will be changing your basic function into an advanced one, but you are not going to notice much difference between the two functions. By changing your function, you are going to be giving yourself the ability to do what the advanced functions allow such as accepting a pipeline input. But, before you can accept these inputs, you must change your parameter to use the parameter attributes.

Example:

```
foreach ($computer in (get - content - path C:\
computers.txt)) {
trial - connectivity -systemname $_
}
```

You should notice that a valuefrompipeline parameter has been added along with a process block. The process block is vital when you are wanting to accept any kind of input from the pipeline. The valuefrompipleine attribute is one of the two ways that you are going to be able to accept information from the pipeline in PowerShell.

Chapter 7

Using Pester with Powershell

You may trial your code after you write it or modify it. But, you will be surprised that there is a high number of environments where trialing is still done manually. A developer will make changes to their code and then run a trial on their computer before deploying the code. However, this type of trial is not going to scale the entirety of the code. Developers will be able to trial a small portion of their script that they created or a function they updated. But, what about the bigger pieces of code? The modules that are composed up multiple PS1 files that rely on a variety of modules?

Automation is going to be the answer to trialing your code.

So, what is pester?

Pester is a community-based project that was designed o trial the framework for PowerShell code that is written in PowerShell. It is an open-sourced project that will allow you to look through the source code and make modifications to it. Pester is going to be able to be used with PowerShell 2.x up to PowerShell 5.x on Windows 10, 8, 7 and Vista. You can also use it with all versions of Windows Server 2003 through the most up to date one. It is even compatible with PowerShell 6.0 Core on a Linux or Mac OSX platform.

Types of trialing

Unit trialing: Unit trialing will be the code by a developer and are usually going to focus on code that was just created or modified. The developer will be provided with feedback on the code to see if it runs the way that they want it to. The unit trialing will be done in isolation. By isolating the trial, they are going to know if they get any errors they will not be caused by an outside force.

To achieve isolation, unit trialing will use the concepts known as mock. The mock is going to be used instead of using the actual external function that you want.

Example: If you are using the code known as path-trial and want to authenticate the existence of the file. If you were to use the actual calling of the path – trial function then you are going to experience several issues with the trialing.

The first thing that you're going to do with your path – trial is that the cmdlet needs to have a bug in it that you do now knot about. The next thing is that you are going to need to assume that the path that holds the file is always going to exist as part of the trial. Issues are always going to arise should the directory vanish unexpectedly. Lastly, the drive that holds the file may not be present or and you should make sure that there are not any issues with the network connectivity or hardware that you are using.

If any other issues happen, then the developer will have to debug the code while also dealing with the other ways that the path – trial cmdlet could have failed.

Integration trialing: This will be the next step in trialing your code. After you have completed their unit trials, they are going to be ready for the integration trialing. Integration trials move past trialing the code that the developer has finished working on and trialing it as well as any related code.

Example: You have updated two functions in module A. This module is going to be part of a bigger project that includes two other modules.

As the integration trial is executed, it will trial all three modules. This is to make sure that any changes in module A do not adversely affect the other two modules.

Usually, integration trials are not going to use mocks. To fully trial integration along with your code, you need to execute that code against a variety of other modules. These modules can be modules you purchased or that are provided to you by Microsoft. Integration trialing is usually called white box trialing. While talking about white box trialing, you may hear references such as clear box or glass box which means that the trialer is going to have access to the very bottom level of the source code.

A lot of source code control systems are going to perform integration trialing automatically. After the code has been checked, it will automatically execute the trials that you have configured.

Acceptance trialing: This trialing will be done by someone who is not the developer. There are a couple companies that have internal organizations that are set up to perform this trial.

Acceptance trialing is usually done in what is known as a black box style. In this style of trialing, the trialer will not have access to the source code, and they cannot look at the source code. Instead, they are going to execute the script and observe the results. Should the results be what is expected, then whatever the code is meant to do will be executed which means the trial will pass.

When you should trial

Most of the time, these trials are going to be done against what the code is supposed to do. It is possible to think that your code is going to pass every time, but you'll be surprised to find out that most of the time, there are going to be an unexpected bus in your code that are found when you go through a trial. On top of that, the creation of these trial is going to provide you with a new base for trialing any updates to your script.

Another time that these trials will be helpful is before you write your script. This is where the term "trial-driven development" comes from. TDD is going to happen when you start by placing your requirements into a document. From there, you will create a trial for every requirement on your list. In addition to that, you will have to make sure that you are creating trials for the failures that occur. Say for example your requirement is for a file fro a website to be downloaded every day at a specific time. The first thing you need to do is make sure that you trial for successful downloads. You need to also trial for a download failure so you can ensure your code can do everything that you require when it comes to error handling.

TDD is going to help you answer the question of "are we done yet?" If you trial for every requirement and your trial pass, then your requirements will have been met which means that your development is complete.

To make sure that you are properly doing the trial-driven development, you need to have requirements that are clear, good and documented. This is vitally important! You should not skip this step!

Your automation strategy is another critical step you should not skip when it comes to your corporation's infrastructure. It does not matter how big your script is; you need to trial it, so you are not causing trouble for your company.

Running trials

Before you can start writing your trials, you need to know how to run them. Pester module will invoke the invoke-pester function. With this function, you will provide the name of the script and the trials needed to execute it, or the name of the folder where the script is. Even though the script is not required with pester trials, the file should end in .trials.ps.1. While this is not a requirement, you will usually create trial files for every ps1 file that you have. This extension is going to allow you to execute every trial in the folder by invoking the invoke – pester function and passing in the name of a directory.

```
$dir = 'C:\ PowerShell \ pester - demo ' Invoke -
pester "$dir\ asicpester. Tests. Ps1"
```

If you wanted to, you can use invoke – pester $dir, and it will run every file that ends in .trials.ps1. You can also run invoke – pester which will cause it to run all the .trials.ps1 files in the folder.

The First Trial

This trial is going to be simple.

```
describe 'basic pester tests' {
It 'B test that should be true' {
$true | should - be $true
}
}
```

The first thing that you should notice is that the pester commands are nothing more than PowerShell functions. Therefore, the describe method is going to be the initial method that is called upon .pester is not going to follow the naming conventions that other PowerShell cmdlets follow. Most, even when you write them, are going to use the verb-noun naming convention.

You should remember that Pester is its own language which makes it easier for you to read the trials. This concept is known as DSL or field Specific Language. DSL is a Code: that is going to make code easier to understand and read. Pester implemented DSL so that the trials were easier to read and could convey a clear meaning.

Basic pester trials are always going to describe command. This function is going to act as a container for one or more trials. Once describe has been put into the code, then a text string is going to describe what the trial contains.

At the end of the lie there is an open squiggly brace, and then the next line is more code which you are going to find until you hit the closing squiggly brace. When you first glance at this code, it is going to look like every other built-in PowerShell command like foreach. But, this one is a little bit more deceptive because you are defining the code block as you pass it into the pester module describe.

```
$scriptblock = {
it 'B test that should be true' {
$true | should - be $true
}
}
```

This script is going to work, but it makes reading the script a little more difficult which can be avoided for your pest trials.

Pester does have another implication that you need to be aware of. In a foreach block, you will have the ability to place open squiggly braces on the same line as the for each line. Both of these scripts are valid.

```
foreach ($xx in $list) {
#place your code here
}

foreach ($xx in $list)
{
#your code here
}
```

This is not going to be allowed when it comes to a pester trial because the script block is going to be considered a parameter of the describe function. Now, if the brace was on the next line, PowerShell would not find it and would return an error assuming that there was no parameter. So, if you want to, you can place a line continuation character at the end of your open squiggly brace, but this is not going to aid anything when it comes to how readable your code is.

Now that you have seen how the describe function works, you are going to be able to create the code block and hold more than one trial on it. This trial is going to be defined by using the function it. Like the structure for the describe function you have to first pass into a string that holds the name of the trial. This is going to be followed by the code block holding the trial condition. Make sure you are saving your code at the beginning of this part in the folder you created.

For this type of trial, you need to execute the same kind of equation, comparison, and function so that you get a boolean value.

The results are going to be piped into a pester should function. The first thing you need to supply is the switch ha indicates the expected results. The -be switch will tell the program what is being pulled into the should equation and what it needs to be equal to pass the second parameter.

Once you execute the trial and look at the results, you should see that the describe section is saved into your file. You need to make sure it is saved before you try and execute the invoke function.

You should get results that say what was executed, a description section and how long the trial took to be executed. At the very bottom, you will see how many times the trial passed or failed.

The failure

What is your code going to look like if it fails? Let us take our original code and modify it, so it fails.

```
describe 'should exist test' {
it 'should exist' {
'C:\powershell\ pester - demo \ invoke -basicpester tests.ps1.' |
should -exist
}
}
```

The description in this script block is set up so that the trial will fail. Passing the boolean to fail in the should compare that to true and cause the trial to fail. Whenever you run the trials, you are going to see a result that tells you where it failed and how many times it failed. Your results for this trial should be mostly in red because the trial failed.

Allowing more than you should

```
describe 'should exist test' {
it 'should exist' {
'C:\powershell\ pester - demo \ invoke -basicpester
tests.ps1.' |
should -exist
}
}
```

There is a wide assortment of the should function. Another function you can use is the -exist switch. This function will take the name of the file that is piped in and see if it exists.

You will find that this is useful when you are trialing functions that need to be downloaded or creating a file. It will also be useful when validating your code. So, if you were to write a module, one trial you would run is to check the existence of your manifest file. Since you are working with PowerShell, you will need to use PowerShell code as part of the trial.

```
describe niibe 'should exist with variables test' {
$sotomefile should exist" {
$somefile | should exist
}
}
```

The file that is being trialed is going to be put in the variables place. This is going to allow you to use a string interpolation so that you can make the documentname part of the name that you gave to the trial. From there you are going to be able to reuse the variable passing it into the should function. At this point, the file name will be part of the trial name. You are going to know exactly which file is being trialed which makes the results more valuable.

Pester context

There are often that a describe block is going to contain multiple trials. This is going to be a helpful group so that you can put related trials into the same block. This will be where you are going to use the context function. You should think of the context function as a sub describe function. It is going to provide an extra layer of result for your code.

```
describe 'grouping using context' {
context 'test group 1 boolean' {
it 'should be true' { $true | should - be $true }
it 'should be true' { $true | should - betrue }
it 'should be false' { $false | should - be $false
it 'should be false' { $false | should -befalse
}
context 'test group 2 - negative assertions' {
it 'should not be true' { $false | should - not - betrue }
it 'should be false' { $true | should - not - be $false}
}
ocntext 'test group 3 - calculations' {
it '$xx should be 45' {
$xx = 45 *1
$xx | should - be 45
}
it 'should be greater than or equal to 22' {
$yy = 2 * 11
$yy | should - begreaterorequal 22
}
```

```
it 'should with a calculated value' {
$yy = 2
($yy * 11) | should -begreaterthan 20
}
}
context 'test group 4 - string tests' {
$testvalue = 'arcanecode'
#test using a like (not case senstive)
it "testing to see if $testvalue has arcane" {
$testvalue | should -belike "arcane*"
}
#test using cLike (case sensitive)
it "testing to see if $testvalue has arcane" {
$test value | should -belikeexactly "arcane*"
}
}
context "test group 5 - array tests' {
$myarray = 'arcanecode', "website"
it 'should contain arcanecode' {
$myarray | should -contain 'arcanecode'
}
it 'should have 3 items' {
$myarray |should -havecount 3
}
}
}
```

While that is a lot of trials in one block of code, each trial is going to be executed and you are going to get a result of what happened with every trial. Each trial is going to be broken down into groups as they are in your code block so that you are able to see what is happening in each code block and how long it took to see if the result was accurate or not.

Using the context function is going to make it so that the results are broke up easily for you to read. Let's look at the results that you should have gotten from running the code.

trial group 1 is going to show you the trials that are performed at the beginning of this code block. But, if you want, you can use the shortcut should – be $correct and use the -betrue switch. The same can be fone for the -befalse switch.

trial group 2 holds a negative pester assertions. Just add a -not switch before the call of the be switch which is shown with the should -not -betrue.

trial group 3 shows how pester is going to calculate the values. On top of that, the be greater switches along with the be fewer switches are going to show you what how high or low the numbers should be. While doing this, you need to enclose your whole calculation in a set of parenthesis. This will force PowerShell to complete the calculation before passing the result to the should function.

Pester is going to support the trialing of string values as you saw in trial group 4. This trial is going to use the like operator under the cover for a wildcard match while one version is case insensitive and the other is case sensitive. While it may not be shown, you are also going to use the be switch for your string comparisons.

In trial group 5, you see that there are some trials for arrays ascertaining to the array containing a specific value while ensuring that the array has a specific count.

There are some common should trials that you are going to be allowed to perform, but it is not a comprehensive list. There are going to be switches that will work with the files, regular expressions and so much more.

Chapter 8

Advanced Pester trialing

The first thing that you are going to need to do is to look at the same location for the demos in GitHub's repository. It is advised that you use the same fold as before so that you do not have to search your computer to see where your files are. However, this is not a requirement. To make it easy, place the product $dir so that you are directing yourself to the demo folder faster.

```
$dir = 'C:\ PowerShell \ pester - demo'
```

Let's play pretend

Before you can run any trials, you need something to trial. In this section, you are going to create a mock function. Below, are some of the basic requirements for this function.

- Accept the name of the file that is needing to be created.

- Look to see if the file already exists. If it does, then you need to input a warning and have the function give you the result of false.

- Read any data from the database and then do the calculations. From there, write the results of the result

- file name that is provided by the parameter.

- Return true so that you know that everything went the way it was supposed to.

To understand mocks, you do not have to create a function that does everything in step three because step three is going to be simulated by using the write-protracted statement.

```
#function to test mocks with
function pretendtodosomething ()
{
[cmdletbinding () ]
param
(
[parameter (mandatory = $true) ]
$outputfile
)
#for the practice purpose, you need to pretend to read something from the database, do calculations, and then create a file
$first, you need to check and see if the target file exists and if so, inform the user and exit the function.
Write - verbose "checking to see if $outputfile exists."
$exists = test-path $outputfile
if ($exists)
{
write - warning "output file $outputfile already exists!"
return $false
)
#you are going to pretend that the write-verbose statement contains a long, complex series of code.
#in a non-demo situation, the code we care about is going to be the code in our testing section
write -verbose 'pretending to read data located in the database.'
write-verbose 'pretending to do calculations'
write-verbose 'pretending to write out results to a new file.'
return $true
\
```

In the first trial, you have to create a unit trial as you did earlier.

```
$exists = test - path $outputfile
```

The trial path is going to be a PowerShell cmdlet. To get the isolation principle, you will need to replace it with a mock call.

Integration trial with $trialdrive

With isolation trials, you are going to be using a mock function, so you are not executing the code in a code base like Powershell. After that, you need to do integration trialing. Integration trials are going to allow you to execute all the code that you are working with even if it was not written by you. But, you will need to eliminate any permanent effects which means that you cannot leave any evidence that you ran the trials so do not leave any stray files or any records in a database.

Starting with the database, you will need to use a database that is listed on a trial server that has a known state. You want to do this so that you know exactly what records are in the database before you do the trialing. This is a known state called the gold copy. Once you've executed the trials, you will be allowed to examine the state of the database by comparing it to the gold copy to make sure you are getting the results you want. You should authenticate any changes that were made to the database so you can restore it to its original state.

Whenever you are eliminating effects to your file system, pester simplifies the system for you. Instead of having to clean up the files, pester has a variable called $trialdrive. Whenever pester runs a trial, it is going to generate a temporary area on a hard drive for the trial to be carried out and from there that location is going to be placed in the $trialdrive variable. Inside your trials, you are going to be able to reference the $trialdrive variable in the same way that you access the $dir variable.

```
#write-verbose "pretending to write our your result to
the file $outputfile
write-verbose "really writing your results to the file
$outputfile
"some text was written at $(get-date)" | out-file
$outputfile
```

While this is just so you can see what the code is going to look like, when you run the trials, you will need to put your actual code in here. But, you are still not ready to run your integration trials. Sadly, the script for the unit trial has been broken. Using the out-file will end up violating the isolation trialing rules so you will have to add it to the list of mocks in your original unit trials. So, let's revise your code.

```
#test 2, ensure your function is returned as true
should the file not exist.
#create a test-path indicating that file doesn't
exist.
Mock test-path { return $false}
mock out - file { }
$calling with verbose can aid in testing
$testresult = pretendtodosomething
$filethatdoesn'texist -verbose
it 'returns true if the file does not exist and
processed ok' {
$testresult | should -betrue
}
```

As you can see you are going to use the mock out – file cmdlet. Now that the unit trial is being run in isolation the function will pass. This shows a good point in if you change the code you are trialing; you will be changing all of your trials.

```
describe 'integration tests' {
#create your file
$mytestdata = "$ ($testdrive) \ mytestdata.txt"
$test using the file that does not exist
$testresult = pretendtodosomething $mytestdata
it 'returns true if the file does not exist and
processed ok' {
$testresult | should -betrue
}
it 'see if the output file $mytestdata now exists" {
$mytestdata | should -exist
}
}
```

Let's add the code to an integration trial.

You describe block will use the name integration trials appropriately. The next line will reference the pester built-in variable known as $trialdrive. From here, you will call two trials. Make note that you are not using any mocks so you will need to use the trial – path and out – file cmdlets in your function to get it actually to be executed.

The first trial will be you passing the file name that does not exist. The $trialdrive location is created on your hard drive the first time that it is called don from the describe function. It will stay that way until the end of your script block. You should also be assured that the documentname that holds the $mytrialdata variable will not exist. This variable will be passed onto the pretendtodosomething function. From there it should as it should be get past the trial – path, therefore, writing the file using the out – file and then be returned to you as true. The next trial will use the should – exist function and switches to authenticate the file that was made.

An integration trial area is going to make it so that both your trials pass. On top of that, you are going to see the long path that includes the GUID in the name for the second trial. Should you decide to go find the file on your hard drive, you are not going to find it. The instant that PowerShell found the closing squiggle pester deleted the trial drive folder.

```
describe 'integreation tests' {
# create a file name
# $mytestdata = "$ ($testdrive)\mytestdata.txt"
#create a file name (revised)
$mytestdatafile = 'mytestdata.txt'
$mytestdata = "$ ($testdrive) \ $ ($mytestdatafile)"
#test using the file name that does not exist
$atestresult = pretendtodosomething $mytestdata
it 'returns true if file does not exist and is not
processed ok' {
$atestresult | should -betrue
}
#it "see if the output file $mytestdata now exists" {
# $mytestdata | should -exist
#}
#exist test revised to show only the file name
it "See if the output file $mytestdatafile now exists"
{
$mytestdata | should -exist
}
#added test to see if the file exists
$atestresult = pretendtodosomething $mytestdata
it "returns false if $mytestdatafile existed" {
$atestresult | should -befalse
}
}
```

The first thing that you see is that the product is declared to hold the name of the file. The $mytrialdata variable was revised to the $trialdrive and the new $Smytrialdatafile variable. The next trial revised to just show the file name and not the entire path or file.

Lastly, another was added to the trial for when the file already exists. The file was created in the first trial so it could be used in the second trial to check to see if it existed. Your result is going to show you the results from all three trials.

Acceptance trials

Acceptance trials are going to accept your code and make sure that the results are left behind for you to examine whenever you want. So, any files that are created will be left at the end of the trial, unlike an integration trial where nothing is left behind.

```
describe 'acceptance tests' {
#setup a location and file name
$dir = "C:\ powershell\pest-demo'
$testfile = 'acceptancetestdata..txt'
$testfilepath = "$dir\ $testfile"
#ensure the file isn't left over from the previous
test
if ($ (test-path $testfilepath))
{
#delete it, do not ask for confirmation
remove - item $testfilepath -force -erroraction
silentlycontinue
}
#test using a file name that won't exist
$atestresult = pretendtodosomething $testfilepath
it 'returns true if file does not exist and is not
processed ok' {
$atestresult |should -betrue
}
#test for the existance of the output file
it "see if the output file $testfilepath now exists"{
$testfilepath | should -exist
}
$atestresult = pretendtodosomething $testfilepath
it "returns false if $testfilepath existed" {
$atestresult | should -befalse
}
}
```

The trial is going to start by setting aside a folder that already exists with a file name. Note: this does not use the $trialdrive folder.

From there it will check to make sure that the file exists having been left behind from the previous trial if it is then it is deleted. Then all three trials are going to be run, and you will receive the results from those trials.

Chapter 9

Abstract Code – Tree

By now you probably know that PowerShell is a language that is automated. PowerShell is also known for the fact that it can create active directory users, exchange mailboxes, move files, and tons of other things all in one program without having to worry about not having the tools that are going to assist you in making your job easier.

The first thing you have to do to make all of these actions be executed is to write the script, and writing script can be complicated depending on what it is that you are doing. While you are writing them, it is easy to forget that there is a particular order that your script has to follow. Essentially, every script you write is going to be able to be broken down into multiple components. These components are functions, variables, conditions, so on and so forth. You may not realize what is going on because it looks like nothing more than a lot of text that you have placed in a file, however, your code is going to be placed in a specific order so that it executes properly. This order is going to be shown in PowerShell by use of the abstract Code: tree (AST)

Your AST is comprised of the .net namespaces that are going to break your code down into the most logical components. Parsing the script in this manner is going to give you several benefits that you may not have noticed before, like locating all of your variables, any functions that have been declared, so on and so forth. You are not going to need this each time that you use PowerShell necessarily, however when it comes time that you do, AST makes sure that you are working with a clean solution rather than having the code that looks messy and is hard to follow.

In this example, you will first see PowerShell to parse the script.

Example:

```
function do - something {
boarder ($name)
}
Do - thing - header 'tool.'
Write out - text 'is this thing on?'
```

Now when you parse this code, you need to insert the parse file method on your object.

Example :

```
[System.Management.Automation.Language.Parser]:ParseFi
le('C:\Script.ps1',[ref]$null,[ref]$Null)
```

With this step parsing your script, your code will now be broken down into the logical components.

```
PS C:\> $ast
Attribute { }
Use of statements { }
Argument block
Start block
Process block
Block end
Function do - thing {
boarder ($header)
}
Do - thing -header -tool
Write out - message - is this thing on
Dynamic argument block
Requirements for script
Extent
Function do - thing {
Argument ($header)
}
Do - thing - header - tool
Write out - message - does this thing work.
Parent
```

Rather than having a lot of text in your code, your script is going to be parsed to just the important components. After the code has been put into this format, you are going to do some modifications to it. For example, if we wanted to find any function declaration that is inside of the script, you are going to use the find all () function technique.

Code:

```
PS C:\> $AST.FindAll({$args[0] -is
[System.Management.Automation.Language.CommandBaseAst]
},$correct)
```

Every function is going to be able to pull the call inside and modify the search before locating every variable that is inside as well as changing the object type.

Code:

```
PS C:\> $AST.FindAll({$args[0] -is
[System.Management.Automation.Language.VariableExpress
ionAst]},$correct)
```

Every component that is in your PowerShell script that is listed under the system management automation language namespace. To look at every option type that is available to you, you will hit the table key while on your PowerShell console. Several of the objects are going to be found, but it is not going to make sense instantly. Despite that small issue, you should still try the objects out in your code just so you can see how they work and what is going to be returned to you. In doing this, you are going to locate functions and variables along with variable types, parameters for functions and a lot more than you will be able to use.

AST is a complicated topic, but it is one of the few things that you are going to want to use and learn by trial and error. After you have gotten the basics down, you are going to be able to expand the knowledge that you possess and parse all of your scripts.

Chapter 10

JSON and Powershell

While the world around us is constantly overtaken by software, those who work in the IT field are going to have a front row seat to how software is taking over our world because they work with the software-defined programs that are replacing everything that we know. One of the biggest components that you are going to want to focus on with your software is the constant adaptation of the DevOps applications. Any of these services are going to need to communicate so that they can provide a path for the programs and users to interact with them and make them work as they need them to work. This is where you are going to want to use an API.

What we are going to be looking at is the rest API that is going to send back data whenever searched. It is this data that is going to come in the JSON format normally. JSON is one of the methods that you can use to structure your data so that the software can intake the data properly. While working with PowerShell, you are going to have tools at your disposal so that you can work with JSON. One of the tools is going to change your data from JSON, and the other can change it from JSON. These commands are going to work quickly with the rest APIS or a great number of other services where a return and be sent out or accepted in the format of JSON.

Let's look at these two commands and see how they are going to work.

The JSON is going to work with the rest API or any other service that you may want it to work with.

Example

```
{"employees":[
 {"firstName":"John", "lastName":"Doe"},
 {"firstName":"Anna", "lastName":"Smith"},
 {"firstName":"Peter", "lastName":"Jones"}
]}
```

It is in this example that you are going to be showing the objects of the employees with the array and there are going to be three objects listed inside of that array. At this point, we are going to assign the string variable inside of PowerShell.

Example:

```
$employees = '{"employees":[
 {"firstName":"John", "lastName":"Doe"},
 {"firstName":"Anna", "lastName":"Smith"},
 {"firstName":"Peter", "lastName":"Jones"}
]}'
```

If you just read the string, then there is not going to be a lot that you can do with it. There is no way that you are going to have the capabilities to extract specific employees without using a string manipulation which is going to extend your code and get messy. Instead, you are going to use the JSON data and turn it into a structured object. Once all of the objects have been made in PowerShell, you are going to use the change from – JSON code on the $employees code.

Once you have done that, you should see that the object is in a position that is going to make it easier for you to parse the object. However, when you perform the task for each employee on the list.

Code:

```
$employeesObj.employees | foreach { $emp = $_; Get-
AdUser -Filter "(givenName -eq '$($emp.firstName)') -
and (surName -eq '$($emp.lastName)')" }
```

Using the change command for JSON, you are going to have the option of changing any piece of code for JSON straight into the PowerShell object. However, you do not have to do this if you do not want to. You can take your object and send it to your rest API or any other selected service where JSON data is required. For this, you are going to use the change to command.

To use the change to command, you are going to be doing the opposite of what you were doing with the change from command. Your command is going to pull your object and change it into a JSON string. But, with your data in this form, you cannot truly work with the object in PowerShell. You are typically going to use this command when you need to manipulate the object before working with a pure source of JSON code.

Your change to and change from JSON commands are the only two commands you are going to use when working with JSON in PowerShell.

Chapter 11

Automating a SQL Server

Your job can change at any time. Your boss could come up to you and say that you need to work with a server that is running off of SQL and it needs to be up and ready to be used by everyone by Friday. While this is going to sound like something that you are not going to be able to accomplish, you are going to be able to. Before you continue, you are going to need to figure out where the ISO for the SQL server is. In this section, you are going to learn where that ISO is and how you can use SQL with DSC.

Thanks to PowerShell and DSC you are no longer going to have to write out long scripts that are going only to execute a simple task. Thanks to DSC, you are going to have the ability to write the configuration for a task and have it applied across a single server, or several servers at one time. Thankfully, Microsoft has made it to where DSC resources are going to work with SQL servers, and you should take advantage of that!

You need to ensure that you are working with PowerShell version 5 for this strategy. It was with this version that DSC was improved upon thanks to updates. The first step is to make sure you can create a configuration with DSC. To do this, you are going to use the optional configuration data since the SQL server is going to require proficiencies. You do not have to set out the specifics for an option that is going to enable plain text proficiencies through the configured data. Instead, you are going to have to set certificates that are going to work with your proficiencies.

You can create a configured data file and place all the information that you are going to need to enable the plaintext passwords for the DSC MOF file as well as the node that is going to apply to this configuration.

Example:

```
@{
AllNodes = @(
@{
NodeName = '*'
PSDscAllowPlainTextPassword = $correct
},
@{
NodeName = 'localhost'
}
)
}
```

With your data configured, you are going to move on to create the DSC configuration.

This code is going to hold every bit of script that is going to represent the SQL server and what it is going to look like when it is deployed. You need to open a text file and copy and paste all of the code into it.

Code:

```
#necessary -Version 5
Configuration SQLStandalone
{
 boarder(
[psproficiency]$Setupproficiency ## Need to pass a
proficiency for setup
 )
 Import-DscResource -Module xSQLServer
 Node $AllNodes.NodeName
 {
 feature
WindowsFeature "NET-Framework-Core"
{
 Ensure = "Present"
 Name = "NET-Framework-Core"
 Source =
"\MEMBERSRV1InstallersWindowsServer2012R2sourcessxs"
}
xSqlServerSetup 'SqlServerSetup'
{
 DependsOn = "[WindowsFeature]NET-Framework-Core"
 SourcePath = '\MEMBERSRV1InstallersSqlServer2016'
 Setupproficiency = $Setupproficiency
 InstanceName = 'MSSQLSERVER'
 Features = 'SQLENGINE,FULLTEXT,RS,AS,IS'
 SQLSysAdminAccounts = 'mylab.localAdministrator'
}|
xSqlServerFirewall 'SqlFirewall.'
{
 DependsOn = '[xSqlServerSetup]SqlServerSetup'
 SourcePath = '\MEMBERSRV1InstallersSqlServer2016'
 InstanceName = 'MSSQLSERVER'
 Features = 'SQLENGINE,FULLTEXT,RS,AS,IS'
}
 }
}
```

As you can see in the code, you are going to see comments that are going to tell you various things about the code that are going to make it easier for you to understand. There is the possibility that the code does not make a lot of sense to you at first. However, it will begin to make more sense to you as you learn more about the DSC and practice it with your code.

Take note of what is on line nine, there is the import resource code, and this is crucial to your code. This is going to bring the SQL module where all of SQL DSC resources that are going to need to be used when you are trying to run the configuration. It is these resources that are going to be easy for you to obtain by downloading them from the PowerShell gallery. You can always open a PowerShell console and be able to determine if your module is the module you are looking for by using this code.

Code:

```
Find - module - name xSQL Server.
```

You may also notice that version 2 is available for you to use by installing the find module to the install module.

Code:

```
Find - module - name xSQL Server | install - module
```

You can now verify every bit of the SQL Server with the DSC resources that are made available through the program.

Code:

```
Get - dsc resource - module x SQL server
```

After you have built the configuration, you are going to create a MOF file for your node so that the server has something to be installed on. To do this, you are going to use a dot source with the configuration that was built on the session that you are currently using which is going to make the DSC configuration that is available a stand-alone for SQL.

When you execute the configuration, it is going to create a MOF file for your server which is going to be installed with the SQL Server on the DSC. With the MOF file, you are going to call on the local host. Of which is going to hold all of the instructions that you need to for installing the SQL server to the machine that you are using.

Code:

```
Start - dsc configuration - wait - force - path C: SQL
standalone protracted
```

When doing this process, it is going to take quite some time to complete since it is installing the entire SQL server. As long as it runs into no issues, the server is going to tell you that you need to reboot your system or it is going to reboot automatically depending on the reboot settings.

And that is it. You are done. You have no successfully installed the SQL server. When you use the appropriate configurations, you are going to be able to go through this process multiple times over making it easier and easier each time that you do it.

Conclusion

Thank you again for purchasing this book! I hope this book was able to help you to learn some more advanced functions that you are going to be able to use in Powershell.

The next step is to start using these new functions that you learned. Learning the advanced functions of PowerShell will make it to where your PowerShell programs are going to be top notch, and you are going to be able to add more depth to them for your users. You will notice that your PowerShell programs are going to be easier to execute because PowerShell is going to automatically make decisions based on the attributes you input into the program. Powershell is going to become easier knowing that you are not having to work against the program, but with it!

Do not get frustrated with yourself when you find that writing PowerShell code is a bit confusing because it is that way no matter what kind of coding language you are writing. It is going to take time and patience to fully understand PowerShell code, but it will help you out in the long run because once you get the hang of PowerShell, you will be able to master any other language out there!

Finally, if you enjoyed this book, then I'd like to ask you for a favor: Would you be kind enough to leave a review for this book on Amazon? It'd be greatly appreciated!

Thank you and good luck with your PowerShell journey!

Made in the USA
San Bernardino, CA
28 May 2019